Breakthrough to Fluency

Breakthrough to Fluency

English as a Second Language
for Young Children

EDIE GARVIE

BASIL BLACKWELL · OXFORD

ISBN 0 631 93970 9 (Paper)

0 631 17110 X (Cased)

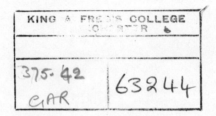
Printed in Great Britain by
The Camelot Press Ltd, Southampton

Contents

Foreword

The main purpose of this book is to offer some guidelines to teachers concerned with young children whose mother-tongue is not English. It is hoped that the work may also be of help to teachers of West Indian children and English speakers who customarily use dialects other than standard English. In addition teachers who work in nursery schools may find some of the ideas helpful.

The book is the outcome of several years of teaching, teacher training and research in the field of English as a Second Language, but it reflects in particular the author's recent experience as coordinator of language work in the Bradford Infant Centres. The rather specialised situation which exists in Bradford, where non-English speaking children of Asian background are given a period of orientation and language help before entering the first schools, has provided insights both into the problems of the young second-language learner and into the implications for education which are worth considering by all who have to provide for these children. Their learning needs are the same whatever the circumstances of their learning.

The author wishes to acknowledge with grateful thanks the tremendous amount of help and inspiration received from the staff and children in these centres and from those in the first schools, with whom she worked closely for three years. She is also indebted to the Bradford Authority for permission to use materials in this book which were originally written for Bradford. In addition she would like to thank those colleagues in Birmingham and elsewhere who have given helpful comments and advice in general.

It has to be admitted that reflection on the many issues which the first chapter attempts to highlight, suggests more and more that the ideal situation would be to offer the non-English speaking child his early education in his own language. There is some evidence from research on bilingual education to show that this produces the best results in the long-run. It is, however, probably impossible for many reasons to carry out this practice in most parts of Britain at the present time. We are therefore left with the problem of providing an educational environment which will help the young child to develop his basic concepts and to tackle the first steps towards literacy and numeracy through the medium of English as a Second Language.

Given this situation it is incumbent upon us to make sure that the second language does become a flexible tool for the child. The notion, still unfortunately prevalent in many areas, that the five-year-old will somehow pick up this tool by simply being exposed to it in the limited period of his school day demonstrates a singular lack of understanding about the function of language in the learning process. A considerable amount of help must be given if the second language is to become for many children more than a pidginised lingua franca for day-to-day communication reflecting the dialect of the local peer-group.

It is realised that the approach suggested in this book would probably involve a fair amount of reorganisation and adaptation of cherished practices in the present system, and much more research is needed before firm lines of action can be stipulated. However, it is hoped that the suggestions advanced can be adapted to suit the needs of teachers working in many different situations and it is hoped that these ideas will give food for thought, not only to practising teachers but also to those who train them and to those who are responsible for the policies of the future. It is hoped also that for the hard-pressed teacher the techniques with which the greater part of the book is concerned, will be helpful here and now with the continuing problems with which she is faced.

There is no suggestion of a language course. It is felt that in these early years the second language is best taught in and through the normal activities of the school curriculum. But this demands that the teachers fully understand what it means to have to speak a new language in order to learn whilst learning to speak the new language. It is in an attempt to foster this awareness that the book has been written.

Edie Garvie

1
Language and Learning Across Cultures

Introduction

So many books have been written about human language from so many different points of view that the reader can become completely bewildered and can begin to wonder how, in the first place, a person ever acquires his own language and how, in the second, the learning and teaching of a second language can ever proceed. Verbal Language is one of the most miraculous abilities of the human species, the one which divides it from all other species. It is also one of the most fascinating areas of study.

All teachers should be both interested and knowledgeable about language as it is such a vital component of the learning process. The links between thinking and speaking are close and complex and the growth of concepts is helped considerably by the use and ordering of words. Teachers who are concerned with children learning in a second language should be particularly aware of this and especially skilled in techniques which will help the children with their difficult task. But the first essential is for the teacher to have some sort of framework for her thinking about language. What is it? And how is it learnt?

In a book of this kind it is impossible to give anything but a brief treatment of this enormous subject. Teachers are advised to read further for themselves and some suggestions are given at the end of this chapter. However, something can be said briefly which will help to highlight the task for the second-language learner, particularly the very young learner, and all that this implies for the work of the teacher.

About language

Language is a means of communication with others and it is a means of communication with oneself, a tool of thinking. It can be heard, spoken, read and written. It consists of sounds and symbols divided into words and groups of words which reveal a particular order and system according to certain rules. It can alter in subtle ways according to the ability and state of the user, the purpose to which it is put and the situation in which it is used. These things may be expressed as follows:

LANGUAGE

Is:	*A Means of Communication*		
	(a) with others		
	(b) with oneself—a tool of thinking		

		Received	*Produced*
Can be:	*Oral*	Heard	Spoken
	Graphic	Read	Written

Consists of:	(a) sounds and symbols
	(b) words and rules for patterns
	(c) groupings of words and rules for patterns

Is affected by:	(a) ability and state of user
	(b) purpose to which it is put
	(c) situation in which it is used

We have to be conscious of all the above factors when we consider the learner's task. For communication with others and with himself the learner has to acquire knowledge of all the' basic aspects of language and the teacher, bearing in mind the limitations of his ability, must provide appropriate experience to help him.

About the acquisition of the first language

All normal human babies are born with the physical organs and the mental capacities for the development of verbal language and the particular language they eventually acquire is that of the home and specific community into which they are born. In other words the acquisition of language is the result of the interaction between endowment and the factors of environment. Which has the greater influence, a question which has taxed scholars over the years and which is still a source of controversy, cannot be dealt with here. It is important to remember that both play a part in the acquisition of language and to consider what this can mean for the child learning a second language.

As the baby grows he begins to sort out the world about him. From the confusion of things, movements and noises, certain ones become clear and associated with his own particular needs. He becomes aware of his own body and what he can do with it. He begins to recognise his father and mother and other members of his immediate family who administer to his needs and over whom he realises he has a certain amount of control, and gradually he learns to order his environment while at the same time he learns to recognise certain verbal signals and eventually to imitate them for himself. As understanding develops so also does language which progresses from cries to babbling and then to one-word utterances which gradually expand into longer sentences. By some miraculous process of analogy and generalisation the child finally arrives at the stage when he has mastered the basic systems of the language of his community, its sound patterns and the rules for patterning words and sentences. He has also mastered, and this is important, rules of usage relating to the purposes and situations with which he has become familiar in his particular community. It is a never-ending source of wonder that all this has become well developed in the normal child of any community between the ages of four and five.

What must be emphasised is that the child's language develops along with his growing concepts of things, people, events and the system of values and behaviour which this particular language expresses. This is his culture which has claimed him for his own and, no matter how far he may move away from it, it will continue to influence him to some extent for the rest of his life.

About learning a second language

The above very brief description of mother-tongue acquisition

3

highlights the vital links between thinking, speaking and culture. It also highlights the fact that a person's first language develops step by step with the early development of his physical body and the maturation of his brain and nervous system. For this reason the mother-tongue is very special and very much a part of the individual.

When we come now to look at the learning of a second language these two things in particular have to be remembered. Even as the expression system differs from that of the mother-tongue, so also do the patterns of thought and culture which go with it. The learner comes to the learning of his second language as a developed being, even at the age of five. He will never again be in the position of the baby acquiring language as part of the general maturation process. So his second language can never really be for him the very personal possession which is a marked feature of the mother-tongue, particularly if the latter continues to be the language of his home and most intimate affairs while the second language remains only the medium of school. In these circumstances the second-language learner has to be specially motivated to learn his second language.

We can now look at the nature of the task which confronts him. As with the acquisition of the first language he has to learn a particular inventory of sounds, an increasing number of words and a set of rules for structuring those words. At the same time, if he is to use this expression system meaningfully, he has to learn the patterns of thinking and culture which go with it.

In one sense the task is the same as before because the learner is again learning a language and all languages consist of sounds, words and structure, geared to thought and culture. But in another sense the tasks are different because of the new being the learner has become as a result of his cultural background and first language. He has, for instance, learnt to think and form concepts and he knows inherently what language is and can do. So he is in a different position from the baby whose task is still that of learning to think while he acquires his language. On the other hand the very culture and language which have put the second-language learner ahead of the baby in maturation, bring him a stumbling-block; again putting him in a different position but this time affecting the task in a negative way. All the time the learner is trying to understand and use the second language, the ways of thought

4

and expression of his first language keep intruding and 'interfering' with his learning. So the learner needs help and tuition.

The situation for the second-language learner is in fact often like that of a person who is trying to decipher a message by using the wrong code. He has to be helped in the first place to crack the new code and later to switch codes when the circumstances arise, without confusing the two. This idea of cracking a code will be taken up again later in the book.

So far the task of the second-language learner has been looked at in a very general way. Are there some steps of progression which can be pinpointed? One useful way of looking at this, remembering the important link between the growth of concepts and language whether first or second, is to consider the *steps* of concept development in terms of the second language. Though cultures may differ in their concepts of the world there is a certain amount of overlapping and the actual steps which the mind goes through are probably universal.

There is first of all the need to identify and label, at a simple level, the object, person or event being experienced. The second step is to be able to qualify what has been identified, to express attributes of size, colour, shape, purpose etc. Third the learner has to have ways of expressing relationships of various kinds and fourth he needs terminology for classifying or identifying sets.

These things the young child gradually learns to handle in his mother-tongue. The second-language learner has to go through all the steps again but in the new code. Even an adult second-language learner has to do this. He should be able to do it quicker because of his maturity and the fact that he has already done it in his mother-tongue, though of course there will be 'interferences' of learning to offset this. The following somewhat contrived example may help to illustrate the processes involved.

IDENTIFICATION (perceiving and recognising)

This is a gerbil.

QUALIFICATION (noting things about it)

It is small/fawn.

5

It has a long tail.
It eats X, Y and Z.
It lives in X, etc.

RELATION (comparing and associating)

It is like a mouse.
It is different from a squirrel.
It is bigger than a field mouse.
It is smaller than a water-rat, etc.

CLASSIFICATION (recognising the set)

It is a rodent.

The steps give a clue to the kind of language devices needed, whatever the particular language being used by the thinker. Here they are illustrated by English but French, Urdu or Chinese could have been used equally well.

The 'tion' ending of the four keywords for the processes makes a useful reminder. And yet another keyword should be added. The young child acquiring his first language goes through this process over and over again as his experience of both physical and social environment increases. As it increases so his ability to think logically and to solve problems also increases along with his power over language. He can, for example, use longer sentences with more elaborate structure and he can handle the devices for expressing such things as cause and effect and possibility. In other words he acquires the ability to manipulate his thinking. This gives us the fifth 'tion' and adding it on to the previous list we might say:

MANIPULATION (using concepts to produce more elaborate ideas such as cause
and effect and possibility)
It (the gerbil) does not drink much water because it comes from a hot country and
there is not much water in the desert.
      or
If we let it out of the cage it might get lost or the cat might eat it.

The second-language learner, who may well have reached this stage in his mother-tongue, has to work up to it again in the new language and has to be given the means of expression.

6

So perhaps we can say that we now have at least a rough framework for the task of the second-language learner. He has to work through the five 'tions' in every area of the experience to which he is exposed where he needs his second language. Gradually, as he goes along, he learns the appropriate words, structures and rules, not forgetting the sounds of the language. It is important to remember too that the *means* of learning which he used in acquiring his mother-tongue, things such as imitation, analogy and generalisation, are available to him again. The difference is that he now has to be helped and motivated into using them and indeed if the language has to be learnt quickly for the purpose of learning other things, then the whole framework of his learning must be taken in hand by an understanding and knowledgeable teacher.

The young second-language learner at school

The normal five-year-old child is already a thinking and speaking individual. When he comes to school he has moved along the road of concept development to some extent and he can express himself accordingly in the manner of his own culture and language. The task of education is to foster what he comes with, to help him to develop and extend further and to lead him on to the skills of literacy and numeracy.

For all young children the first experience of school has a strong impact. At best it is stimulating and pleasurably exciting; at worst it is shattering and terrifying. For the child from a home where the culture and language match those of the school the first is more likely to be true but for the child from a different culture whose language does not serve the purposes of the educational system, the first experience of school can be a bewildering nightmare. All the familiar landmarks have suddenly disappeared. The safe and cosy world in which the child has been cared for and in which his concept of himself as part of that world had grown to the point where he could confidently take his place in it, has suddenly fallen about his ears, leaving him defenceless, vulnerable and sometimes very frightened.

One way of describing this phenomenon is to speak of culture shock. It has often been discussed in the literature concerning immigrants arriving in a new country, as are many of the older children in our schools. What is not appreciated sufficiently is that children born in

Britain can suffer just as much in this respect if their background differs from the culture of the school. In some ways the problem of the five-year-old is possibly greater than that of older children or adults because his development as a person has not yet travelled very far. He is still struggling with his basic concepts of life and his confidence in himself as part of society is still very new and shaky. Then, just when he needs school to help him extend his conceptual development and increase his confidence, he finds himself in a situation where everything is suddenly very different and life for a time becomes completely disorientated.

That so many children not only survive but seem to thrive in these circumstances is a tribute to many sympathetic and resourceful teachers and to the resilience and adaptability of the human being. But we are still left with the problem of those children who carry the scars of this intial school experience for the rest of their time in the first school sector and perhaps beyond. We are also left with the problem of those who may appear to be settling down happily, who learn to communicate in the language of the school to some extent and to join in the various activities and who even learn to read and write in a mechanical way, but who at the same time fall further and further behind in the matter of realising their full potential. In other words the initial progress may be more apparent than real. The remedial classes in junior and secondary schools are full of these children, out of all proportion to the numbers of second-language learners in the schools. There is surely something wrong somewhere and the chances are that the trouble starts in the first stages of school. The child's first teacher has a tremendous responsibility.

The teacher and the problem of learning 'interference'

The teacher is faced first of all with helping the child to cope with his early bewilderment. With usually no means of verbal communication and perhaps little understanding of the background from which he comes, she has somehow to convey to the child that she cares for him and that school can also be a place where he can be happy and confident. This goal established she has to begin the business of trying to extend and develop his learning, again with little understanding very often of the particular form his previous learning has taken. Nor can she

8

make discoveries about this through, for example, pleasant conversation about home incidents or discussion of objects, apparatus and pictures in school. Child and teacher do not share the same code and verbal communication is not possible.

In these circumstances it is all too easy for the teacher to make wrong assumptions. She could, for instance, treat a bright child fluent in his own language as though he were an empty vessel with no concepts or language at all, or she could assume that all small children have the same understanding of life and the only problem is one of learning a different way of expressing it. Perhaps the most dangerous assumption of all is to believe, that given a rich environment with a flow of the second language going on all round them, these children, by some extraordinary process of osmosis, will pick up enough of the way of thought underlying the second language and the expression system itself, to enable them to profit by the educational curriculum in the same way as the indigenous children who have been thinking and speaking this way for several years.

The first thing the teacher has to be aware of is that cultural and linguistic difference means that there will be 'interference' of learning and that this calls for a very special contribution from her if the target culture and language are to be absorbed and used for the child's development in school. This may involve in the beginning taking the child virtually back a stage or more in his conceptual progress so that he can travel the same road again by means of the new code. We saw how the second-language learner has to go through the 'tions' all over again. It may also mean that some withdrawal of second-language learners from normal school situations is necessary so that this special work can be done adequately and without hindering the fluent indigenous speakers. This can be done within the school itself or by establishing separate centres. There are varied ways of handling both situations. Local authorities and schools themselves will have to decide what is best in their own particular circumstances.

However the methodology is managed the teacher must be constantly aware of the things which may be puzzling the child so that she can smooth the way for his development to proceed. This means that she must make a special effort to educate herself about the problems of her own particular pupils.

9

Some examples of the 'interference' problem

The problem of 'interference' of learning can appear in many guises, sometimes springing from conceptual misunderstanding, sometimes from differences in the expression systems of the languages involved, and sometimes both. Take, for example, the area of house-play. The teacher might be involved with a group of Punjabi-speaking children and there may be a tea-party in progress. Remembering to help with language the teacher would perhaps point to the milk-jug and sugar-basin and give the children the English names, asking them to repeat the words after her. The children would no doubt do this quite happily and efficiently but they would be puzzled by the use of the objects in the play. What the teacher had not realised is that in the homes from which these children come tea is made and served differently. The tea, milk and sugar are all put into the kettle and brewed together. Here we have an instance of words being given for a concept which does not exist for the learner.

Another example comes from water-play. A child whose first language is Urdu may tell his teacher that the water in one vessel is shallow and that in the other dark. The teacher will duly correct the child and ask him to say 'deep' instead of 'dark' which again the child will do but once more with a puzzle left in his mind. In his language there is one word 'gehra' and it can refer to what is meant both by dark and deep in English. The child has to learn that there are two terms in English when his own language has only one to cover the two ideas and he has to learn further when to use which.

The child who says 'aeroflane' or 'vindow' is experiencing 'interference' from the sound system of his own language which may have sounds not quite the same and/or a different way of using them. In certain languages, for example, some sounds can appear only in the middle of a word and never at the beginning. Some languages do not have consonant clusters such as 'scr' in English. A speaker of such a language will say 'iscratch' or perhaps 'sicratch' to make things easier for himself.

Sentence and word structure can also reveal 'interference' difficulties. The Urdu speaker who says 'I not coming' may be confused by the fact that in his own language the presence of 'not' sometimes allows the equivalent of 'is' to be left out, and the one who says 'My castle is big than yours' is following the custom in Urdu where the adjective itself is never altered as English alters 'big' to 'bigger'. Another word is put in to do the same job.

The ways languages differ in the devices which they use to express the same or similar concepts is revealed again in the 'he/she' and the 'yesterday/tomorrow' confusions which some teachers constantly meet. It is not that the learner does not perceive the distinctions of sex or time. It is simply that his own language uses different devices to make these distinctions, such as using different verb endings to indicate male or female and saying something like 'one day away in the past/future' to say what English expresses by the one word 'yesterday/tomorrow'.

Sometimes, too, the second language contains words which sound similar to words in the mother-tongue but which mean very different things. For instance the word for 'in' in Punjabi sounds like the word 'under' in English. One can readily see how bewildering this must be for a child, who automatically reacts to that particular group of sounds as he has learnt to do in his own culture.

Perhaps these few examples, mostly concerning one mother-tongue, will serve to point up the kind of things which the teacher must become knowledgeable about if she is to help the second-language learner sufficiently. As a result of this knowledge she will be better able to see where most time should be spent and which aspects of the second language need special practice. She will also gain some pointers for her techniques. She would not, for example, introduce the English words 'in' and 'under' at the same time to a Punjabi speaker.

Before we leave 'interference' of learning something must be said about the kind which comes from the learning of the second language itself. When a child says, 'I comed in' for instance, he is making the wrong use of a rule he has learnt. This *is* a way of making past tense in English but it is inappropriate for the verb 'come'. It is a stage which the second-language learner probably has to go through even as the indigenous English child had to and teachers should be pleased to discover that the child is making analogies and is therefore on the way towards productive use of the language. What they must also remember, however, is that the English-speaking child is likely to have gone through this stage at least a year earlier, again suggesting that

11

special intensive help is needed for the five-year-old second-language learner if he is to catch up with his indigenous peers in his use of English, the tool of learning.

If we consider once again what was said about the nature of language at the beginning of the chapter and see it now in the light of all these possible 'interference' difficulties we begin to have some idea of the enormity of the task which faces the learner of a second language if this is to become as fluent for him as his first, and something little short of this is required for the second language to be an adequate tool of learning. What the teacher must somehow be able to do is to help the child not so much to unlearn what he has already acquired but to go through the steps again, using the things he has learnt about language and what it can do, to show how another language belonging to another culture can do similar things and perhaps some particular things of its own. She must also help him to see that this in no way casts aspersions on his first language and culture. It is a matter of having two codes, each of which is appropriate for its own purposes.

The dialect speaker

This last point has a specific significance for teachers of West Indian children and children whose dialect is different from the language used in school. The problems of children from completely non-English speaking homes are experienced to some degree also by children who speak a non-standard dialect of English also reflecting a certain amount of cultural difference. They too have problems of interference both of concept and language and they also can be bewildered by the initial impact of school with its different values and expectations. A West Indian child, for instance, who has been taught to sit still and be quiet, has difficulty in understanding the kind of freedom he is given in the first school. Fear of this can make him withdrawn or in some cases obstreperous, neither of which condition is conducive to learning.

The problem which is particularly acute for these children is that they can quickly develop an inferiority complex about the kind of English they speak and teachers must be prepared for this. It is all too easy to give the impression that the child's language is sub-standard and wrong and that he has come to school to have it corrected. The child and his

12

culture are blamed in a subtle way for being inadequate and impoverished. The teacher expects little from the child who therefore gives little and possibly ends up by becoming the eternal behaviour problem, classed as remedial and remaining so till he leaves school.

The first essential for the infant teacher is that she should learn to understand the dialect speaker. She must spend as much time as possible with him in situations of real communication and must do everything possible to show him that he is understood and accepted. If the child speaks a dialect of English this should not be so difficult, especially if the teacher comes from the same part of the country. But if the child is West Indian this may call for a special effort because his way of speech can differ quite extensively from standard English. The interested teacher is referred to the books and resources suggested at the end of the chapter for information about this. Much depends on the part of the West Indies from which the family came originally and it must be remembered that there are differences amongst the West Indians themselves. Also, if they have been settled in Britain for some time, the chances are that the West Indian Creole has been overlaid by the British dialect of the area where they live, so the problems are confounded. In general the main problem of the West Indian speaker is that while he shares his vocabulary with the speaker of standard English, his pronunciation and the ways in which he constructs his sentence can be very different. Not only does he have a difficulty of oral communication but he also has trouble when he comes to learn to read because books are written in standard English and unless the child is familiar with this he cannot read fluently as he is having to 'translate' all the time. It is worth considering in passing that the dialect speaker may even have a more difficult problem here than the non-English speaker simply because his language *is* English but not the English of books.

Conclusion

Whether the child is non-English speaking, West Indian or British dialect-speaking, it is necessary for him to learn the common code of the school which is as good a way as any of defining standard English. What the latter certainly does not have to be, is BBC English, Queen's English

13

or public school English. There is no element of 'speaking proper' in this at all. It is a matter of the smooth running of a community. All should be able to use the shared code when it is needed and the business of education is made easier if they can.

So the onus is on the young child's teacher to set the right scene for all that follows. The ways of coping adequately in the same class with non-English speaking children, West Indian and dialect speakers would form the topic of a book in itself. Each of these groups has its own particular problems but they do have in common the problem of adjusting to a school community which has a different set of norms and means of communication from those to which they are accustomed. It may be that by aiming in this book to cater specially for the needs of the non-English speaker, we shall at the same time be able to highlight the general problem.

Whatever the source of difference the child needs firm guidance and tuition, particularly in the beginning, so that the common code is acquired as quickly as possible, and techniques for the teacher in this respect are described in later chapters. The next chapter outlines an approach which provides a general framework.

Further Reading

Britton, J. *Language and Learning* Penguin Books Ltd. 1970
Craig, D. *An Experiment in Teaching English* Caribbean Universities Press—distributed by Ginn 1969
Wilkins, D. A. *Second-language Learning and Teaching* Edward Arnold 1974
Wilkinson, A. M. *The Foundations of Language* Oxford University Press 1971
A Language for Life Report of the Committee of Inquiry appointed by the Secretary of State for Education and Science under the Chairmanship of Sir A. Bullock, FBA, H.M.S.O. 1975, especially Chapters 4 and 5
Concept 7–9 E. J. Arnold and Sons 1972
Immigrant Children in Infant Schools Council Working paper 31, Evans/Methuen 1970

Teaching English to West Indian Children The Research Stages of the Project. Schools Council Working Paper 29, Evans/Methuen 1970

2
A Possible Educational Approach

Introduction

It is suggested in this chapter that learning is a matter of both making discoveries and forming habits. It is also suggested that learning progresses from that which has been associated with particular limited situations to that which has been generalised and become productive for the learner over an increasing range and complexity of situations. The approach described in this chapter is based on these two ideas. They suggest an educational practice which provides a field of learning appropriate both in kind and extent where the learner has the opportunity to explore and find out things for himself. At the same time there is a certain amount of direction and focus so that what is discovered can be monitored, practised and consolidated. They suggest also that the learning field should become gradually wider and more elaborate as the learner becomes more skilful and begins to use his learning creatively. This kind of approach is now considered in relation to the young second-language learner.

Field and focus

(a) *The field*

The total learning environment of the school including the flow of language the child is hearing all round him constitutes the field in which he must make his discoveries. This environment includes the areas of the curriculum such as pre-reading, number, story, music and all kinds of creative work, with their various activities and materials which are part of the normal school day. It also includes, and these are just as

16

important, the everyday activities of assembly, playtime and dinner-time, and special events like visits and open days. Language plays an important part in all this. The entire experience *and* the language to which the young child is 'exposed' is his field of learning.

The central idea of this book is that discovery type learning, important as it is, is only one part of the matter. On its own it is not sufficient to ensure true and lasting learning. The teacher must help the child to focus upon the field of learning. What does this involve?

(b) *Focusing by the teacher*

If the teacher is to help the child to focus she must first do some focusing herself, so that she knows what exactly are the things she wants the child to discover. It will be necessary to examine the field very carefully in order to highlight the learning purposes and the activities and materials involved. The teacher must discover the function which language plays in all this so that she can help the child to link it very carefully to the experience.

The most effective means of achieving this is to draw up a checklist of language used in all the situations the child will face during the school day. This list will be constantly referred to and frequently modified but its use will serve as a guide to each child's progress. The work of studying the language used and then drawing up the checklist is probably best done as a team activity. The team leader, who may or may not be the Head, initiates it, and there should be frequent meetings so that adequate time is given for discussion and the pooling of ideas. New techniques of analysis may also be suggested and tried out. It may be that different people take responsibility for different parts of the curriculum and act as leaders in their own particular parts of the field. For example one person might concentrate on mathematics and work carefully and methodically on the learning content, the activities and materials used and the language which all this demands. She would then share her findings with the others in the team so that all could benefit. Each area of the field might be covered in this way, including general activities such as events in the dining-room, cloakroom etc. The resultant language checklists when combined, would make an extremely useful guideline.

Equipped with such a guideline, and it must be stressed that it would be *only* a guideline and not a syllabus, the individual teacher would be made more aware of the language content of the child's learning and indeed of the things about the language in general which the second-language learner has to assimilate. The more the teacher had to do with the making of the guideline the better her awareness. The more she has focused on the learning field for herself the easier she will find it to help the child to do so. There is no suggestion that the teacher should carry the checklist about with her and teach directly from it. The list is for her own study and she should become so familiar with it that its use would become automatic and implicit in all her work with the children.

But it might be helpful to have a copy of the complete checklist on show in the staffroom for quick and easy reference and/or to have the relevant parts of it on the wall beside the various activities so that the adult, in working with the children, could be reminded at a quick glance, of the language possibilities in the particular activity concerned. Sometimes the aim would be to teach new language, sometimes to revise and sometimes to check progress. A useful idea which might be tried is to decide as a team what particular language is to be taught or revised across the activities during the course of a week perhaps and to put this up in several places as a reminder. The checklist is a flexible instrument which can be used in any number of ways.

(c) *Focusing with children*

In working with children a variety of methods should be used. It is possible to focus with individual children or with groups and the groups can be large or small. The number of adult helpers can also vary. It all depends on the purpose of the operation. In the early stages, for example, when the children's English is so poor that there is little means of communication between teacher and children it is beneficial to have several helpers who can act as foils for one another. This is described later in the book. It is a way of helping children to see what is expected of them. Later the number of helpers can be reduced as the children themselves become able to take a more verbal part in the proceedings.

(d) *The individual*

Focusing with individuals should take place when the children are working on their own with equipment or playing by themselves with play apparatus in the hall. The informed adult will help by supplying or eliciting the appropriate language as and when it is needed. There are times also when the child working with materials needs constant guidance and language help. The child should be discovering both concept and its means of expression. In addition, the child should also be discovering that certain language is useful across a variety of situations. For example instructional language such as 'Begin here', 'That's right' and 'Do you understand?' has very general application. But if the child is to grasp this quickly the teacher must learn to control her instructions. She must remember to use the same language for the same situation each time it occurs. There are, of course, many different ways of saying 'that's right' but it is important in the early stages that the child should be offered the same formula each time. Too much variety in the beginning can bewilder a child and hinder the main purpose of the learning activity.

In fact the child is having two kinds of language focused for him at the same time. There is the language which is needed for the particular learning in hand and there is that which is general in many activities including everyday communication. This is what is meant by speaking a second language to learn while learning to speak the second language itself. The latter is being used to further the growth of concepts and the activity of learning the concepts is used as a vehicle for learning further language. It is a two-way process.

Supposing, for instance, the activity is one of bead-threading where the child has to thread a lace to a given pattern, the teacher would make sure that the child could use the words 'bead' and 'lace' and the names of the colours involved. She might also concentrate on the sentence, 'I'm/you're threading beads' and perhaps. 'This bead goes next'. The words 'same' and 'different' could be given and the phrases, 'the same as' and 'different from'. All of this language is relevant to the task in hand. At the same time, things like the pattern in the sentence, 'I'm threading beads' (subject—verb—object), the 'ing' ending to give the present continuous form, the 's' on 'bead' to indicate more than one,

19

etc., are all examples of aspects of standard English which are used over and over again in all kinds of situation. The knowledgeable teacher is aware of what she is doing here. She might even make some effort to point up these things so that the child really 'encounters' them. He could, for instance, be asked to repeat a bit of language several times, though the teacher must beware that the main purpose of the activity is not lost.

Focusing in this way is useful with all children but for the non-English speaker something more is required. The discoveries which he is making are somewhat shaky and in need of consolidation. His attention is divided between understanding the concept and learning the language that goes with it and, as we have seen, there may also be 'interference' of learning from his own culture and language and/or from his previous learning of English. The child needs time for pause and assimilation. It is as though the work of the normal school day were a fast film. The film has to be stopped occasionally to allow time for its content to be properly absorbed. To some extent the teacher can do this while the child is working amongst the other children but as we saw, too much of this spoils the film and the overall continuity is lost. What is required is further focusing away from the general buzz.

In a quiet corner or preferably in another room altogether (and how important it is in every school to have such a place) the work done in the normal situation should be gone over again with the use of a variety of techniques. It must be remembered that the main aim here is to help the child to consolidate his learning. He should be given opportunities to use what he has discovered, to imitate and practise the language. In addition the variety of technique and apparatus should aim at helping him to move on from sheer imitation to spontaneous use of language, and eventually to creative use by the process of analogy and generalisation.

For instance in the bead-threading activity the sentence, 'I'm threading beads' might go through the following steps:

IMITATION

Teacher (as the child is working): Say, 'I'm threading beads.'
Child: I'm threading beads.

20

SPONTANEOUS USE

Child (on another occasion when he has chosen the same activity and with no prompting from the teacher): I'm threading beads.

CREATIVE USE

Child (in another situation and again with no prompting from the teacher): I'm drawing men.

It must be stressed that the final stage is not reached overnight. It may be a very long time before progress is shown and there may be none at all if the teacher does not help to make it possible. Let us look a little more closely at what the child is doing here. First he is simply repeating the series of noises made by the teacher. To move from this stage to the next, he has had to understand the association between these noises and the activity. The next stage requires that he sees a pattern emerging, one which can be used again with different words slotted in. Furthermore he has also to become aware of the component parts of the pattern and of how some of these can break down further. The use of the 'ing' ending taken from 'threading' and put with 'draw' illustrates the point. Finally in this instance he is demonstrating his knowledge of the plural. He did not say 'mans' which would be a quite understandable analogy and a possible intermediate step. He knew that the plural of 'man' is irregular.

If these are the things the child has to do, what can the teacher do to help make them happen? Continuing with the same sentence for illustration we can envisage the teacher first of all concentrating on the bead-threading activity itself. The material would be taken into the withdrawal room and the child would repeat the activity he had been engaged in previously, but this time the teacher would focus much more and get the child to practise saying, 'I'm threading beads'. She might introduce (if she has not already done so) the question, 'What are you doing?' This and other question forms are very useful teaching aids as well as being important language in their own right. It is worth spending time, with the cooperation of other adults, focusing on them so that the child recognises the cues and knows how to respond.

In addition to the bead-threading activity the teacher should gather in the withdrawal room a number of other materials already familiar to the child and so the pattern can be shown to be useful in other situations.

Note that it is important that the work spills over again into the normal classroom situation when the child is working once more with these other materials in the usual way. Further than this, other people can be brought into the operation so that the child learns to change 'I'm' to 'You're' to 'He's', etc. Once this is accomplished pictures can be used of different people doing things and the question asked, 'What is he/she doing?'

Another helpful technique is to use a story or a song where the pattern is constantly repeated. More will be said about this in a later chapter. Devising these aids should be an important part of the teamwork in a school. There should be a large repertoire at the disposal of the teacher, based on the language checklist which in its turn is based on the activities of the learning field.

(e) *Groups*

Useful as a one-to-one relationship between adult and child may be, there are times when it is beneficial to work in groups, both from the point of view of economy of time and effort and of the stimulation which can come from social interaction. Again group focusing can be done within the normal classroom situation and in withdrawal. For instance, it is possible to envisage a small group of children working with one or more adults round the nature table, discussing the names of the objects and their properties. This labelling is very important and much time and patience must be given to it especially with non-English speaking children. Later, the same group in the withdrawal room could look at pictures of the objects, again listening to and practising the labels along with structures such as, 'This is a——'. They might also place cutouts of the objects on a magnet board, commenting on their actions as they did so, and they might say rhymes and sing songs about them.

As children become more and more familiar with the school situation and more fluent in the second language, focusing in withdrawal should become less necessary although it should continue to be used for work that causes real difficulty. Focusing within the normal classroom, however, must continue indefinitely. Provided there is sufficient adult help it is useful to have someone acting as a monitor for the non-English speaking children when new materials are being discussed and

22

instructions given, just to be sure that they are following and that the fast 'film' is not causing bewilderment.

The idea of a monitor of experience is further illustrated now as we go on to look at focusing in large groups. This may seem like a contradiction in terms. It is usually easier to focus when the numbers are not large and it is recommended on the whole that this practice be followed. However, there are times, particularly in the early stages, when community focusing is useful. Song sessions and movement sometimes with music can often be used for special focusing, for instance. Another activity which might be explored more in this connection is role-play. In Chapter 5 this is described as 'a community happening'. It involves several adults working as a team, some to act, one to monitor and the others to guide the responses and general participation of the children. The aim is to match very deliberately and slowly certain selected experience and language.

For instance the scene might be a shop or a doctor's surgery or a bus, each of which suggests its own particular language. It is important that only those situations which the children will have met be used here so that the focus is on things already familiar in a general way. Of course role-playing can be done in small groups and much successful work of this kind takes place every day. But the large group activity, particularly in a school where this seldom takes place, can generate its own excitement by its very formality and apparent seriousness. There is also a strong sense of togetherness which is helpful to children from cultures where this is strongly felt. It gives a feeling of security. Besides there are more people to draw on and this offers much more scope for imaginative ploys.

Phasing in gently

(a) *Some general points*

Not only must the teacher provide an appropriate field of learning with regular periods of focusing upon it so that the child is given the maximum opportunity to make his learning meaningful and lasting, she must also try to ensure that this learning progresses. We have seen something of this already when we looked at the development from imitation to creative use of language. The teacher must be able to match the steps of the learner with experience which will foster his movement from one stage to the next. In other words the learning field should gradually increase and become more complex, demanding ever greater effort on the part of the learner.

What follows now is the fairly brief working out of an idea which is presented only as something to be considered at this stage. It is realised that its acceptance in practice would involve most schools in reorganisation. It also begs many questions. Nevertheless it is hoped that some thought will be given to these suggestions as they may be important and if they are then ways could be found of sorting out the questions and dealing with problems of organisation.

It has been said that learning the second language is probably best helped for the young child by fostering its development in and through the normal curriculum, rather than by attempting to use a special language course. However, it may be necessary to phase the second-language learner more gently and gradually into this curriculum. It may well be that we do many children a lasting injury by submitting them to an elaboration of experience and language which is beyond their powers to cope with in the beginning, both socially and linguistically. They may require a period of orientation and much more understanding of what they themselves are bringing to the school situation so that they may be accepted first for what they are.

Education by its very nature sets out to change. It aims to change the learner in the direction of its desired goals, but the ways in which it goes about this must take into consideration the learner's distance from these goals and start where he is. For some children the distance will be greater than for others. Young children from non-English speaking homes or from dialect-speaking homes, with all that this suggests about different values and expectations, are likely to be further from the educational goals than are the children from homes where standard English is spoken as a mother-tongue.

The question arises of course as to the rightness of the goals in the first place but this is outside the scope of this book. Suffice it to say that given the present objectives of the ordinary school, the initial approach for the children we are concerned about should be one of gradual orientation. Three stages of this are advocated and will be considered in turn. For convenience they are called 'Initial orientation', 'Cracking the code', and 'Breakthrough to fluency'.

(b) Stage 1—Initial orientation

When the child first enters school the main issue may be the cultural difference between a society which fosters the free expression of the individual and one which values conformity to the group and the recognition of one's place in the scheme of things. For a great many of the children with whom we are concerned, community activities are more familiar than individual freedom. There is little tradition of free play and the use of toys and games for educational pursuit. The children are not used to manipulating gadgets or indulging in imaginative play. They do not chat with adults nor do the adults tell them stories, recite rhymes or sing songs to them. There may also be different relationships with different adults and a difference between boys and girls in this respect. How might the first stage of education meet the needs of these differing expectations?

It is suggested that more time be given in the beginning to community activities than to free play, with as many adults as possible taking part, including the parents of the children if this can be arranged. The activities could take various forms such as movement in the hall, role-play and singing. The emphasis here is on doing things together so that all concerned have a real sense of community. In the beginning the school staff would take a large part in the proceedings but they would draw upon others such as parents and people from the minority groups. A kind of pantomime atmosphere would be created in which shy children would be able to relax and feel drawn to take part in spite of themselves. At this stage verbal language would be very limited and what there was would be closely related to action and bodily activity.

In the movement sessions, for instance, the aim would be to do things together, sometimes to music with very little verbal instruction and sometimes without music when the teacher leading the work would give very precise instructions accompanied by bold clear demonstration of what was to be done. The children would see the other adults following and responding to these instructions and would be encouraged to do

25

likewise. This would be an opportunity to begin the teaching of instruction language and to help the children to understand and respond. As instructions became familiar the adults would reduce the amount of help gradually until the children themselves were responding on their own to the words of the leader.

The role-play should be as suggested above in the discussion on focusing in large groups. Again in the early days actions should speak louder than words and the visual element should be bold and clear. It is suggested that the themes for the play should be geared initially to things which the children are meeting in the school for the first time, things such as dining-room and cloak-room behaviour, or even play with some of the large apparatus to which they are gradually being introduced. The aim is to illustrate behaviour patterns linked to a minimum of situational-bound language, the kind which has sometimes been described as survival language because it enables a non-English speaking child to get by in the general sea of confusion.

Community singing should also be linked with action and though words of songs would be used by the teachers the part of language really being focused on here at this time would be basic rhythms. Songs, as we shall see later, are an extremely useful tool for teaching language partly because the music and the language of a community are closely linked and partly because in the slowing down of the sentence patterns demanded by the time of the music, many things which are slurred in quick natural speech are made clear. But here it is the beat which is important and the rise and fall of the tune which goes with it. Nonsense syllables may serve the purpose as well as real words. When words are introduced it is useful to have plenty of visuals which help to tell what the song is all about and sometimes the teachers can mime the action using appropriate clothes from the dressing-up corner and other properties. These should be kept always ready and be easily accessible.

Already it can be seen that while attempting to meet the basic need of establishing a sense of community we are at the same time beginning to meet other needs as well. For instance the lack of verbal communication is being helped by a carefully controlled use of language closely linked with exaggerated, clear movements. The problem of making sense of foreign-sounding intonation and stress is helped by the frequent use of music, and the problem of knowing how to react in strange situations is relieved by the work done in role-play. In fact the overall aim in the activities chosen is to monitor for the children the whole new experience of school, to give them the opportunity to pause and focus so that they can make some sense of the strange new environment around them.

Interspersed with these community activities there should be at this stage short periods of individual play with apparatus such as the climbing-frame, the building bricks and perhaps the sand-tray. But there should still be plenty of adults about to guide and lead if necessary. Some focusing in small groups could begin in a limited way with children who appear to be settled and the emphasis here would be on labelling or identification of things, people and events already familiar in the field.

This then is the Initial orientation stage, a period for becoming gently acquainted with both the experience and the language of school in an atmosphere of very little pressure. The field is limited and there is lots of focusing by staff and children together.

(c) *Stage 2—Cracking the code*

The middle period, as the child becomes familiar with school routines and instructional language, is one of gradually increasing intensity, particularly in the matter of language. There will be longer spells of guided play with more apparatus available and there will be a widening of experience in general so that the overall development of the child is catered for, with appropriate focusing on language in every area. It will be particularly important at this stage to help the children to discriminate and classify and the language focusing sessions will pay special attention to the first four 'tions' referred to in the previous chapter.

During this stage the foundations of the complete range of the curriculum should be laid, with the first moves towards literacy and numeracy. At the same time it is the stage of intense oral language activity. The aim is to help the children to crack the code of the new language, to move from the stage of imitation and the use of situational-bound language to the one of knowing the rules and using them productively, geared to the development of thought which is also fostered by this ever widening experience.

There should be more frequent and longer sessions of small group focusing and the community activities, though perhaps less in number, should concentrate more on verbal language. More and more use should be made of story, rhyme and song with the emphasis on more specific language difficulties. Rhymes in particular are helpful in the matter of pronunciation, stress and intonation. All of this can be helpfully linked with music and movement, imaginative use of pictures and other projected material, tapes, records and perhaps more sophisticated apparatus such as the language master and the synchrofax machine (see Chapter 7). Some interesting work can be done with discrimination of sounds and children can be taught to work on their own with the audio-visual aids, provided there is an adult near to help monitor.

The limited response to simple instructions suggested for the movement periods at the Initial orientation stage should now give way to more complex and imaginative work. There should also be organised games in hall, yard and classroom. These are useful for the teaching of social language such as 'It's your turn' or 'May I go next?' Games such as Snakes and Ladders can be useful now together with those which have cards and pictures like Snap and Lotto, especially if the pictures are carefully chosen to represent things which the children are learning to label in other activities. Such pictures should also be used for pre-reading and number work as they involve visual discrimination, matching and counting. It cannot be stressed enough that the children have to learn their second language *at the same time* as they are learning all the other things the school curriculum demands. It is at this stage when the normal curriculum is really introduced to them and when they have learnt at least to label and qualify to some extent, that the teacher can help the children more by trying to ensure that known language is used when new skills are introduced and that the same patterns are picked up and used in as many other activities as possible.

A useful way of ensuring that patterns are picked up fully is to organise a centre of interest, which is the theme of Chapter 8. A number of areas of the curriculum are selected after a topic is chosen as the central theme. This gives tremendous opportunity for integrated work with language as the servicing agent throughout. It is of course necessary that these centres of interest should be carefully planned by

28

teaching teams and a language checklist is particularly helpful here. It is a useful reminder to all the staff of the language they should be covering in the various areas of the curriculum. Added to this, of course, will be the special language of the selected topic.

The main purpose of this second stage then is to lay down for the children the pattern of early school work while at the same time they are helped to crack the code of the second language. Within a still fairly limited school field they should be able to use the basic rules and patterns of English and they should have a vocabulary of the most common and frequently used words in addition to those which they need for the special purposes of their school activities.

(d) *Stage 3—Breakthrough to fluency*

The final stage of this phasing-in period is concerned with helping the children to adjust to the normal school pace of work. Equipped, as they should be now, with a fairly adequate tool of learning they should be given experience which will challenge and extend them in every possible direction. They should also begin the business of reading and writing to some extent but teachers must be sure that the material they are given can be used by the children orally. It is all too easy for the second-language learner to balk at print and some of them learn to do this very successfully indeed. Tempting as it may be to push children on, it is wiser to be patient and to do everything possible to increase the fluency in oral language which has begun to be possible because of the breakthrough from imitative to productive use of English.

New topics of interest can be introduced in all areas of the curriculum and familiar ones exploited and extended. In connection with the latter, teachers should endeavour to manipulate the elements of the limited situation so that new and sometimes incongruous situations are produced. One sense in children which we often do not consider enough is the sense of humour. For instance a familiar story can be altered in imaginative ways to cause tremendous interest and fun. Or in play such as that in the house-corner, objects can be placed in odd situations.

Also completely new elements should be introduced. Additional utensils can be added to the house, new goods put in the shop or a different sort of shop set up. All of this gives rise to exciting discussion and the need for more elaborate language. Here are two dialogues which might be used in focusing sessions which illustrate the point. First a very simple bit of language following play in the house with a limited amount of material.

Dialogue 1

Mrs. X	Hello, Mrs. Y
Mrs. Y	Hello, Mrs. X.
Mrs. X	Do sit down.
Mrs. Y	Thank you.
Mrs. X	Would you like some tea?
Mrs. Y	Yes, please.
Mrs. X	Do you take sugar?
Mrs. Y	No, I don't.
Mrs. X	Do you take milk?
Mrs. Y	Yes, I do.
Mrs. X	Would you like some cake?
Mrs. Y	Yes, please.
Mrs. X	Would you like a biscuit?
Mrs. Y	No, thank you. I must go now.
	Thank you for the tea. Good bye Mrs. X.
Mrs. X	Good bye Mrs. Y.

Second, a more complex example, after considerable manipulation of the situation to introduce new elements and varieties of the old so that the children have to discriminate and relate, sometimes with things not present in the actual situation, and to use more elaborate language including the special social language needed here.

Dialogue 2

Mrs. X Hello, Mrs. Y. How are you?

Mrs. Y Hello, Mrs. X. I'm very well, thank you.

Mrs. X Would you like to sit on this chair or that one?

Mrs. Y I'll sit here, thank you.

Mrs. X Yes, I think that one is more comfortable. This is my new teapot. Do you like it?

Mrs. Y Oh yes. It's very nice. Your old one was brown, wasn't it?

Mrs. X Yes. I like this one better. It's nicer to look at and it holds more tea. Do you take milk and sugar? I forget.

Mrs. Y Only milk, thank you.

Mrs. X Would you like some cake or a biscuit?

Mrs. Y I'll have a biscuit please. May I have another cup of tea?

Mrs. X Of course. Pass your cup.

Mrs. Y I must go now because it's getting late. Thank you so much for the tea. I enjoyed it very much. Good bye Mrs. X. I hope you will visit me one day.

Mrs. X Good bye Mrs. Y. I'll try to come and see you.

Note that the second dialogue is more like natural conversation, especially in its shortened response forms such as 'Only milk, thank you'. Advanced usage of language is not always a matter of longer sentences. It is also one of knowing more about the devices of style and appropriateness.

There should be by the third stage a noticeable increase in the amount of real discussion and conversation. The children's language should have reached the stage of the fifth 'tion', Manipulation. They should be able to project into the past, the future and the possible and to use words like 'if', 'then', 'so' and 'because'. This gives scope for imaginative play of all kinds. The opposite is also true. Imaginative play gives scope for the use of such language.

During this period some attempt should be made to reduce the amount of aids, both material and human, so that more reliance is put on verbal communication alone. There should be, for instance, more telling of stories without visual illustration and there should be less need for other adults to work with the teacher. There should also be much more opportunity for the children to initiate their own ploys and direct their own learning.

The final stage of the phasing-in period with its accent on fluency should be a rewarding experience for the teaching team whose careful step-by-step work will really now begin to show results. For a long time yet and perhaps right through school these children will need the understanding and help of their teachers but it is those concerned with the earliest stages of education who bear the biggest responsibility. So much depends on their ability to give the children the necessary headstart for all that must follow.

The outside helper

In concluding this chapter perhaps a little more should be said about the 'mysterious' adult helpers who have appeared every now and then in the discussion. No doubt some of those who have read so far will be wondering just where they are to come from and what their relationship would be to the teaching staff.

Clearly much of the work suggested requires more than the individual teacher if it is to be done adequately. In fact it is hoped that schools or authorities acting on the ideas presented here would be able to provide a better than usual pupil/teacher ratio in the early stages. If this were possible then much of the added help would come from qualified teachers. There would also be nursery-nurses, welfare ladies and students on teaching practice who would be there on a regular basis and, on occasion, parents, secondary children and other adults who live and work in the area and/or who come from the communities represented by the children in the school. These too could be invited to help. But it must be stressed that there is no suggestion of 'flooding the school' with unqualified teaching help. The whole organisation would have to ensure that there would be no legal problems of responsibility for children.

There should, in the first instance, be a competent teaching team. This team would be responsible for the project or master-plan. They would have their language checklist, they would plan the techniques of focusing and the materials to be used and they would decide where best to bring in the extra help. For instance in the small-group focusing the helpers might be nursery nurses or students. In the community activities, especially the happenings, parents, secondary children and others could be recruited. The important point to note is that all of this help would be given under the guidance of the teaching team who had carefully planned and rehearsed the proceedings.

How could a school go about acquiring all this help? In the first place a teaching team must be convinced of the rightness of what they are trying to do so that they can put a strong case to the sources of help, sources such as the local authority and their own parent-teachers association, perhaps. The authority could be reached through the Adviser who might be able to assist in several ways. She just might be able to increase the number of teachers. She might also help to contact colleges for student help and secondary schools for children doing courses in Home Economics where part of the requirement is work with children. Usually these young people go to nursery schools and the aim is to train them to become better parents in the future. Perhaps the course could be extended to work in first schools and made to include a more formal educational element particularly with children from minority groups. The fourteen-year-old could be shown how to tell stories and how to play with children in groups and individually so that some focus could be put on language.

The plans should also be laid before the parent-teacher association which should make a very special effort to bring in the parents from minority groups. Those schools fortunate enough to have home-liaison teachers have the added advantage of being able to communicate with parents individually in their homes. But many schools, whether or not they have thriving parent-teacher associations and/or home-liaison teachers, do have a good relationship with parents who sometimes join the morning assemblies and sometimes have the use of special parents' rooms where they can meet for a cup of tea and a chat during school hours. It might be possible to draw these parents in a little further. It might also be possible to turn some of the morning assemblies into community happenings of the kind described in this book.

There are many exciting possibilities waiting to be tried. As was said earlier the details of organisation cannot really be worked out here. The aim is merely to highlight the value of special language work and to point to the necessity for lots of adult help in the beginning. Each school and authority must find the best way of putting these ideas into practice, given that they are convinced of the necessity of this work.

For the interested teacher isolated in the traditional school where colleagues are unwilling to experiment the way is hard. But even she can do something to help the situation. She can, for instance, work on a checklist. She may even be able to have the help of friends in other schools in this respect, at least to some extent, as the activities across schools are not basically so very different. She can also try, as she works with individual children, to focus more on language, guided by her list. Again in her story-telling, singing and movement work she might sometimes try to group the children a little and aim the language content to suit the differing needs. Even if all the children have to take part, the focus in the teacher's mind could be on a particular group perhaps with the more fluent children helping the less fluent. Small-group focusing would be a problem without help but perhaps it would be possible, in the same way that a teacher hears reading while the other children are engaged in play, for a group to be taken for oral work. For example, sometimes instead of the teacher hearing the reading of those who *can* read it might be more profitable for her to play in the Wendy-house with those who cannot read, helping them to gain the kind of oral fluency which leads to reading.

The imaginative, persevering teacher will find ways and means, again granted that there is conviction and dedication to the task in hand. If this book helps to further this conviction it will have served its purpose.

Further Reading

Evans, E. P. 'Aspects of Planned Curriculum Change in an Infants School. And Its Fringe Benefits' in *Journal of Applied Educational Studies*

Garvie, E. M. 'Field and Focus in English as a Second Language: A Construct for Learning, Teaching and Teacher Training' in *English Language Teaching Journal* Vol. XXIX, No. 4, July 1975

Garvie, E. M. 'Language does not "rub off"' in *Times Educational Supplement* 5 February 1971

Webb, L. *Modern Practice in the Infant School* Blackwell 1969

Wilton, V. M. E. 'A Mother Helper Scheme in the Infant School' in *Research in Education No. 1*, Vol. 18, 1975

'FIELD AND FOCUS'

A CONSTRUCT FOR LEARNING, TEACHING AND TEACHER-TRAINING

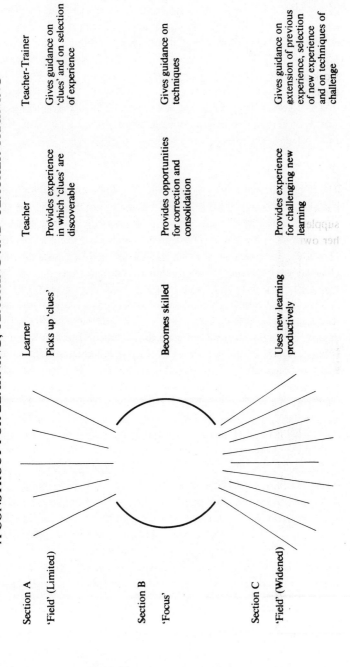

	Learner	Teacher	Teacher-Trainer
Section A 'Field' (Limited)	Picks up 'clues'	Provides experience in which 'clues' are discoverable	Gives guidance on 'clues' and on selection of experience
Section B 'Focus'	Becomes skilled	Provides opportunities for correction and consolidation	Gives guidance on techniques
Section C 'Field' (Widened)	Uses new learning productively	Provides experience for challenging new learning	Gives guidance on extension of previous experience, selection of new experience and on techniques of challenge

3
The Language Checklist

Introduction

The importance of having a language checklist has been highlighted. It has also been said that this should be not so much a fixed syllabus of work as a guideline for the teacher. Not only is it a means of checking the language to be covered but it is also a means of helping the teacher to control the language she herself is using and to assess how far the children have reached in their understanding and use of the second language.

There are checklists in special courses written for foreign and second-language learners which the teacher of young children could use to some extent. The language summaries in the Teachers' Book of Scope 1 (see references) are a case in point. But the teacher must always remember that any course has been designed for a particular group of learners and in catering for her own pupils she must be prepared to adapt and supplement it so that her checklist is really appropriate to the needs of her own situation. It is probably better to start from scratch, making one's own list based on these needs and then later to compare the list with those of others as a kind of double check.

The child's overall need is to acquire the second language as a flexible tool of learning so it is necessary first for the teacher to focus upon the nature of this learning before attempting to list the language items which must be covered. The school curriculum caters for the whole development of the child, the physical, intellectual, social, moral and emotional. Each of these is a broad aim of education and each can be sub-divided into a number of objectives which in their turn give rise to a variety of different activities. While the teacher in the classroom should always be concerned about the broad aims of education her immediate

36

problem is to cope with the objectives and activities, and it is suggested here that she uses these as her starting-point for making her language checklist.

The checklist illustrated in this chapter is one which was made by teachers in the Bradford centres and schools. It is the result of the focusing which was done on the curriculum areas of pre-reading and mathematics. This was a group activity but the same thing could be done by individual teachers in a team, as was suggested earlier. Even the teacher working entirely on her own might begin to formulate a list of the language her children should cover. Combining separate lists into a composite one is a very valuable exercise and the result is not as unwieldy as might be supposed because there is a large overlap of language across the lists in most cases. This was clearly indicated by the work of the Bradford teachers when the lists from the pre-reading and mathematics groups were combined. So much of the language being used had very obvious general application.

It is proposed now first of all to summarise the steps taken by the Bradford teachers towards the production of their checklist and second to look at the framework which was used for making the list. We will then go on to look at the list itself, suggesting at the same time how certain things could have been filled out more and perhaps other things added in the light of further thinking.

The preliminary steps

1. *List the learning objectives, that is, the skills and concepts which underlie the activities the children have to engage in, e.g.*

Pre-reading	*Mathematics*
Visual/motor skills	Relationships
(a) Matching through all stages	Sorting
(b) Discrimination; same/different	Enumeration
(c) Eye/hand co-ordination	(a) Simple recitation of the 'jingle'
(d) Ability to do jigsaws of increasing difficulty	(b) One-to-one correspondence
	(c) Simple naming of the figure
Left/right orientation	(d) Matching the numeral to the group and the group to the numeral
Auditory/speech skills	Conservation
Sequencing	Ordering

37

2. List the activities and materials being used and try to put them to some extent in order of difficulty.

The following is one example from seven pre-reading lists.

VISUAL/MOTOR: DISCRIMINATION; SAME/DIFFERENT

A. Posting box
   (Kiddicraft)

B. Set of 3 objects—2 alike, 1 different
   Use of hoops, sorting boxes, etc. Look for differences of:
   (1) colour (2) size (3) direction of facing
   N.B. The difference must be very obvious.
   All Sorts—Counting Things (E.S.A.)

C. 'Tupperware' Ball and 'Shapes on to Posts', etc.

D. Strip Books: 'Alike and Different'
   (1) 2 strips only—objects (Philip and Tacy) Home-made
   (2) 2 strips only—shapes Home-made
   (3) 3 strips only—objects Home-made
   (4) 3 strips only—shapes (Philip and Tacy) Home-made
   (5) Top and Tail Books (E.S.A.)

E. (a) Set of 3 pictures: 2 alike, 1 different
      Look for differences of:
      (1) colour (2) size (3) direction (4) position
      (5) something left out (6) something added (7) difference of family
      N.B. Match first on to a sheet, then use only separate pictures.

   (b) The Same/Not the Same Pictures (E.S.A.)

F. Discrimination Sheets (Immigrant and Remedial Workshop: Teachers' Centre)
   (1) Match cut-out pictures on to strips of pictures, noticing alike and different.
   (2) Point out which is different from three or four pictures on a strip. If the child is working on his own, a counter can be placed on the different picture. If enough copies are available, the child who has the manual control could colour in the different picture.
   (3) Shapes:
       (a) Colour the two similar shapes the same colour
       (b) All shapes the same colour
       (c) No colour: pure shape discrimination
   (4) Strip books for letters:
       (a) 2 strips only
       (b) 3 strips

(5) Letters on sheets:
      (a) Cut out on card and match on to sheet
      (b) Find the one that is different

G. Memory Games
   (1) With real objects
   (2) Pelmanism 'Find a Pair' cards

H. Picking out hidden pictures from a larger picture,
   e.g. Pre-reading Supplement B (Remedial Department)
      Suitable comics or books.

3. *Use each of these items with children and note the language used, either by recording it on tape or by writing it down as it is spoken. An observer can do it for you. If time allows the same item should be dealt with in this way several times with different children involved.*

Here is an example using one of the items taken from the above list of activities.

TEACHER	CHILD Item E (a)—Colour
Look at these pictures.	
What's this?	It's a ball.
And what's this?	It's a ball.
Yes it's a ball too.	
And what's this?	It's a ball too.
What colour is this ball?	Red.
That's right. It's a red ball.	
Say, 'It's a red ball.'	It's a red ball.
Good. What colour is this ball?	It's a blue ball.
No, it isn't. Look again.	
What colour is it?	It's a green ball.
That's right. And what colour is this one?	It's a green ball.
Yes, this ball is green too.	
These two balls are the same.	
This one is different.	
Show me the different one.	(Child points correctly)
Say, 'This ball is different.'	This ball is different.
These two are the same.	
Put a counter on this green ball.	(Child does so)
Put a counter on the other green ball.	(Child does so)
These two balls are the same.	
Say, 'These two balls are the same.'	These two balls are the same.

39

4. *Do an analysis using all the samples of recorded language.*

This brings us to the second point, the framework which was used by the Bradford teachers for their language checklist. Perhaps the easiest way to show this is to analyse the sample above, as follows:

FRAMEWORK FOR ANALYSIS

Vocabulary	Nouns	Verb parts	Adjuncts	Other structural words
	pictures	look	red	at
	ball(s)	is (what's, it's	blue	on
	colour	and that's)	green	this
	counter	is (by itself)	two	these
		is (isn't)	same	what (what's)
		say	different	what (by itself)
		are	right	that (that's)
		show	good	it (it's)
		put	too	it (by itself)
			again	not (isn't)
			other	a
			yes	the
			no	me
				one (this one)
				and

BASIC SENTENCE TYPES

Statements:

These two (balls) are the same.
This one is different.

Questions:

(And) What's this?
(And) What colour is this ball?
What colour is it?

Responses:

It's a ball (too)
It's a red/blue/green ball.
No it isn't.
That's right.
Yes, this ball is green too.

Instructions:

Look at these pictures.
Say, 'It's a red ball'.
Say, 'This ball is different'.
Say, 'These two balls are the same'.
Show me the different one.
Put a counter on this green ball/on the other green ball.

Exclamations:

None

Some of this language can appear again under Formulae and Rules and Patterns as follows:

FORMULAE

(1) *Concerning the task in hand*
        the same
(2) *Teacher Language*
        Good
        That's right.
(3) *Agreement/Disagreement*
        Yes
        No, it isn't

RULES AND PATTERNS:

(1) Noun plural 's'
(2) Agreement of sentence parts—this one is
                      these two are
(3) Positive/negative—it's/it isn't

In sum then the framework consists of the following headings:

VOCABULARY

Nouns
Verb parts
Adjuncts
Other structural words

BASIC SENTENCE TYPES

Statements
Questions
Responses
Instructions
Exclamations

FORMULAE

RULES AND PATTERNS

41

Let us now look at the language checklist as it appears in the booklet, *Language for the Foundations of Reading and Mathematics* in which the work of the Bradford teachers is recorded (see references).

The Language Checklist

NOUNS

ball, bead, brick, box, button, card, colour, counter, dice, dish, doll, domino, end, game, glass, go (have a), group, half, hole, jigsaw, lace, ladder, line, lot, marble, money, music, name, number, order, pair, peg, peg-board, piano, picture, piece, pile, place, plasticine, rhyme, ribbon, set, shape, side, size, snake, space, stair, step, stick, story, straw, strip, thing, thread, time, tower, tray, tub, way, whole.

VERBS:

add, be, begin, belong, bring, break, build, can, change, clap, come, colour, copy, count, cut, do, draw, empty, feel, fill, find, finish, fit, forget, get, give, go, have, hold, keep, know, let, like, listen, look, make, match, measure, miss, move, must, need, pick, play, point, pull, push, put, say, see, sing, shake, show, stamp, start, stick, stop, take, talk, tell, think, thread, throw, touch, trace, try, use, want, watch, win.

The words listed above had the highest frequency of use by the teachers in their pre-reading and mathematics work. They arise from the needs of the particular learning involved and from the activities and materials, but it can be seen that many of them have much more general application, for example, the nouns 'end' and 'way' and the verbs 'begin' and 'stop'. These two sections of the list are very open-ended, particularly the nouns. Much depends on the activities and materials being used.

ADJUNCTS

Colour

red, blue, green, yellow, black, white, brown, fawn, grey, pink, orange, purple, light, dark.

Shape

round, circular, square, oblong.

Texture

hard, soft, rough, smooth, sharp, blunt.

42

Size

big, small, large, little, long, short, tall, wide, narrow, high, low, fat, thin, thick, deep, shallow, heavy, light.

Quantity

(a) one, two, three, four, five———ten.
(b) once, twice.
(c) many, some, more, less, most, least, several, few, enough, plenty, much, any, each, all, exactly, no, not, else, full, empty, just, every, another, other, both.

Sequence

(a) first, second, third, etc.
(b) next, last.

Position:

Place here, there, top, bottom, middle, centre, side, left, right, up, down, back, front, inside, outside, before, after, out, in, upside-down.
Time now, then, before, after, early, late, today, yesterday, tomorrow, never, yet, still, often, perhaps, maybe, always, ever, again.

Degree

very, too, nearly, almost, quite, only.

State, Manner, Mood

well, sick, poorly, ill, hungry, thirsty, tired, alone, cold, hot, open, shut, clean, dirty, like, alike, same, different, together, altogether, cruel, kind, unkind, greedy, stupid, clever, loud, soft, noisy, quiet, fast, slow, quick, angry, pleased, happy, unhappy, sad, annoyed, cross.

General evaluation
good, bad, nice, pretty, beautiful, silly, naughty, right, wrong, correct.

The teachers' analyses of the words they used suggested the above grouping. The groups vary in the degree to which they are open-ended, ranging from counting words at one end of the scale to those in the section on state, manner and mood at the other end. The latter are very open-ended and can easily be added to. Once again there are words which are particular to the situation and those which are useful generally.

OTHER STRUCTURAL WORDS

1. a, an, the
2. this, that, these, those.
3. I, my, me, mine,
   he, his, him, his,
   she, her, her, hers,
   it, its, it,
   we, our, us, ours,
   you, your, you, yours,
   they, their, them, theirs,
   one (this one)
4. myself, yourself, himself, herself, itself, ourselves, yourselves, themselves.
5. anybody/how/one/thing/time/where,
   everybody/one/thing/where,
   nobody/one/thing/where,
   somebody/how/one/thing/time (s)/
   where.
6. what, which, who, whose, whom, how, when, where, why.
7. and, but, or, nor, so, then.
8. as, than, till/until, unless, while, after, before, if, because, though/although.
9. about, above, along, among, amongst,
   at, behind, below, beside, between, by,
   down, for, from, in, in front of, inside,
   into, near, next to, of, off, on, outside,
   over, past, round, to, towards, under,
   underneath, up, with.

Teachers should be aware of the broad division of words into those which can be described as content words such as the nouns and verbs and many of the adjuncts, and those which are mainly structural or functional. Some of the adjuncts come into the latter category, e.g. 'here' and 'there'. But all of the words listed above under Other Structural Words, are of this kind. They are very important and teachers should make sure that they do everything possible to help the second-language learner in his use of them. Content words are much easier to learn.

BASIC SENTENCE TYPES

Statement:

Gives information, e.g. It is raining.
                              I have a book.
                              Dogs like bones.

Question:

Seeks information, e.g. What are you doing? } The 'open' question with the question word, to which an infinite number of answers are possible.
                          What do you want?

                          Is it six o'clock? } The 'closed' question with no question word with 'yes/no' answer.
                          Do you want some tea?

Response:
Answers a question or acknowledges a remark, e.g. Yes, it is/No, it isn't
                                                   That's right.
                                                    Have you?

Request/Instruction/Command:
Calls for action in another, e.g. Put the light on.
                                         You do it.

Exclamation:
Expresses strong feeling, e.g. Oh, dear!
                                      Well!

Only a few examples have been given. There are obviously many more which could have been listed as each basic type can be sub-divided into a number of patterns. For example, under 'Question' there is the pattern of 'what' with other words like 'colour' and 'size' as in 'What colour is it?' There are also all the other question words, 'where', 'how', etc., with their various patterns. Teachers should think more about this and try to fill out this section. Some suggestions for reading are given. We have already seen how important it is for the learner to see the patterns of the language if he is ever to use it creatively. The teacher must be able to help him so she herself must focus on them.

FORMULAE

Pre-reading and Mathematics Work

the same as
are the same˙
are alike/different
is different from
are just/exactly the same
belongs to/goes with
go/fit together
both the
both of them/them both
how much/many
count the
count up to
as many/much as
more/less/fewer than
bigger/smaller than
the most/least/fewest/biggest/smallest
a lot of/lots of
part of/the whole of
a pair of
in order
in the right/wrong order
comes/goes/next etc.
on top of/at the bottom of
at the side/left/right

Other, e.g. *Greeting and Parting*

Good morning/afternoon/evening/day/night
Hello
Goodbye/Byebye/Cheerio/Tata

Politeness

Please/If you please
Thank you/Thanks/Many thanks/Ta
Pardon/I beg your pardon
Excuse me/Please excuse me

Teacher Language

> Well done!
> Now then!
> Good boy/girl!
> That's the way/right
> Can you tell/show/give me (in this context not a question).

Agreement/Disagreement

> Yes/No
> That's right/wrong/correct/not right, etc.
> I agree/don't agree

Degree of Understanding

> I think/don't think
> I suppose/don't suppose
> I wonder (if)
> I believe/don't believe
> I know/don't know
> I understand/don't understand

These expressions, all of which the young child will hear, if not use at first for himself, are called formulae here to distinguish them from sentences which contain patterns for the child to elicit very quickly, such as 'This is a book'. They have to be learnt as they stand, in the situation for which they are appropriate. Some of them are really quite complex in form and would not be taught to beginners if they were not so useful. The section which shows expressions of pre-reading and mathematics work contains many phrases of very general usefulness. They have been listed here as formulae because they will remain so for quite a while for the second language learner who will meet them at first only in these particular situations. Later he should come to see that they do contain productive patterns. This is also true of some of the other expressions though many of them do remain fairly strict formulae for all English speakers.

Again teachers should try to fill out these sections. These are only a few of the many expressions in the language which we all use frequently and unthinkingly every day. The Bradford teachers found that they were using them during their pre-reading and mathematics work though they were sometimes surprised to realise it.

RULES AND PATTERNS

Nouns

(a) *Singular/Plural*—Three forms of plural with 's', e.g.

dog	dogs (z sound)
book	books (s sound)
house	houses (iz sound)

Irregular plurals, e.g. teeth, men, children, sheep.

(b) Countable/Uncountable, e.g.

	C	U
	pencils	water
	sticks	sand
	glasses	jam

(c) Possessive, e.g. The dog's bone (z sound)

Frank's book (s sound)

Shiraz's hat (iz sound)

N.B. We say, 'The leg of the table' and not usually, 'the table's leg',

(d) Agent, e.g. One who speaks is a speak*er*.

One who teaches is a teach*er*.

One who sings is a sing*er*.

Verbs

(a) Time—Suggested Tense Forms to cover—

Present Continuous, e.g. She is running/eating a bun.

Simple Present, e.g. He walks/does his work.

Present Perfect, e.g. They have arrived/finished their writing.

'Going to' Future, e.g. I am going to swim/drink my milk.

Shall/Will Future (shortened form), e.g. You'll come/take a book.

Past Continuous, e.g. We were going/doing our paintings.

Simple Past, e.g. She went/did her work.

		Continuous Action	*Non-continuous Action*
(b)	Continuity	I am/was speaking	I speak/spoke
(c)	Object	*With an Object*	*Without an Object*
		The second alternative in the sentences above illustrating the tense forms.	The first alternative in the sentences above illustrating the tense forms.
(d)	Regularity	*Regular*	*Irregular*
		count	give
		counts	gives
		counting	giving
		counted	gave
			given

	or
touch	do
touches	does
touching	doing
touched	did
	done

	or
show	go
shows	goes
showing	going
showed	went
shown	gone

Special Irregulars, be and have

be	have
am/is/are	have/has
being	having
was/were	had
been	had

N.B. There are three forms of the regular past with 'ed', which correspond with the three forms of the 's' plural, e.g.

show	showed (d sound)
jump	jumped (t sound)
count	counted (id sound)

There are also several irregular forms such as 'gave' and 'did' shown above and 'met' and 'cut', etc.

(e) Phrasal, e.g. sit down
                 stand up
                 put on
                 take off
                 put up with

(f) Helpers, e.g.

be	as in	I am speaking.
have	,,	I have finished.
do	,,	I do feel happy.
go	,,	I am going to sing.
can/could	,,	I can/could come.
may/might	,,	I may/might come.
will/would	,,	I will/would come.
shall/should	,,	I shall/should come.
must	,,	I must come.
ought to	,,	I ought to come.
let	,,	Let's do that.
dare	,,	How dare you do that!

Adjuncts

(a) Comparative and Superlative, e.g.   Long, long*er*, long*est* (regular)
                                                good, better, best (irregular)
                                                beautiful, *more* beautiful, *most* beautiful (most words of two or more syllables)

(b) Forming adverbs with 'ly', e.g.   quick   quickly
                                    slow   slowly

Sentences

(a) Agreement of Parts, e.g. The *boy is* here. The *boys are* here.

    ┌─────────┐ and ┌─────────┐
    He spoke to *his friends* when *they* came.

(b) Positive/Negative, e.g. It is here. It is not here/isn't here.
                         I have (got) a book. I have not (got) haven't (got) a book.

(c) Nearness/Farness, e.g. This book here is mine. That book there is yours.

N.B. Sentences can be *simple*, e.g. The boy drank his milk.
They can also be more *elaborate*, e.g. The boy in the red jumper quickly drank his milk before he went out.
Note the three kinds of *extensions*—*by word* (quickly)
                                    by phrase (in the red jumper)
                                    by clause (before he went out)
For help with words—see the list of adjuncts.
For help with phrases—here are a few 'time' examples. Teachers should try to list other kinds, e.g. of place.

at two o'clock	on Sunday
at playtime	this/next/last week
at Christmas	every day/time
in March	all the time

For help with clauses—see the list of Other Structural Words, group 8, for clause starters. Some of the question words in group 6 can also be used as clause starters. All of these give suggestions of clause extensions of time, place, reason, etc.

Many more examples could have been listed here but perhaps enough have been given to indicate the order and system in the language and the importance to the learner of acquiring this system. It is economical in terms of mental effort because it means that instead of having to memorise lots of separate items as he has to do with words and formulae, all he needs to do is to learn the rules which can be applied over and over again. There are of course exceptions to the rules and these have to be learnt separately, but the rules are still a powerful part of the language.

CATEGORIES OF EXPERIENCE

School
common objects, materials and activities

Home
common objects, rooms and furniture and activities

Street
shops and other buildings, vehicles, activities

Gardens
Parks and countryside generally

Kinship
the family and relationships

Parts of the Body
and the things we do with them

Articles of Clothing
for boys, girls, men, women; different cultures

Animals
land, sea, air; wild and tame; helpful to men; parts of the animal body; zoo, farm, circus

Plants
garden and wild

Occupations
people who help us

Food and Drink
link with home and shops

Toys and Games
link with school; rules of the game, taking turns

Tools, Utensils and Containers
link with home, school and occupations

Substances
as distinct from things which can be counted

Times and Seasons
clock, calendar, events of the year linked to cultures

Emergencies
things broken or lost, people or animals hurt or lost.

This section was added to the list to offer teachers a source of ideas for topic work. A topic can be 'fed into' the learning situation in any area of the curriculum and it helps to establish a centre of interest (see Chapter 8). The topic will bring with it its own particular vocabulary and perhaps some special formulae also. The special language of topics found to be most useful and common in the infant school could be added to the general checklist. Note that there are, broadly speaking, two kinds of topics, one such as 'the post-office' which is a situational topic, and the other such as 'articles of clothing' which can come into many situations.

Further thoughts

This language checklist emerged from the focusing which teachers did on the part of their field concerned with pre-reading and mathematics. As they worked the ideas grew and so did their awareness of language. The study of grammar books and/or courses for the second-language learner could have produced much the same list, apart from the special language of the curriculum areas studied, but the exercise of working out things for themselves was far more valuable. It is hoped that other teachers reading this book will be encouraged to do the same, though for those who need a quick check now, the list which is offered here may prove helpful. It could be that teachers focusing on other parts of the field only really require to add the special vocabulary and formulae of those areas, because what the checklist here contains is virtually the basic code of the language, and any other study of language about any area at all will also contain this code.

There are, however, two things which the Bradford teachers did not cover in their checklist. One of these is the sound system. This has been very fully dealt with in many books (see references) and it is not proposed to dwell on it here but it is useful for a general checklist to contain the sounds of English as follows:

Vowel		Consonant	
Phonetic Symbol	*Example*	*Phonetic Symbol*	*Example*
iː	s*ea*t	p	*p*it
i	b*i*t	b	*b*ig
e	h*e*n	m	*m*ake
æ	b*a*t	w	*w*ell
ɑː	cl*a*ss	f	*f*at
ɔ	n*o*t	v	*v*ery
ɔː	t*a*ll	θ	*th*ick
u	l*oo*k	ð	*th*en
uː	sp*oo*n	t	*t*op
ʌ	c*u*t	d	*d*og
ə	moth*er*	l	*l*eave
əː	th*ir*d	n	*n*od
ei	p*ay*	r	*r*ope
ou	c*oa*t	s	*s*tep
ɑi	t*ie*	z	*z*ebra
ɑu	h*ow*	ʃ	*sh*oe
ɔi	t*oy*	ʒ	plea*s*ure
iə	d*ear*	tʃ	*ch*ange
ɛə	p*air*	dʒ	*j*am
uə	p*oor*	j	*y*et
		k	*c*an
		g	*g*et
		ŋ	wro*ng*
		h	*h*at

The phonetic symbols are not important but they do help us to remember that we actually use in speech many more sounds than our alphabet would indicate. This part of the code can be practised particularly by the use of rhymes and songs. Two sets of material which are specially useful are Julian Dakin's and Dorothy Aickman's (see references). This material is useful too for practising patterns of stress and intonation which are a very important part of the sound system but are not very easy to list. Again some reading on this is suggested.

Purposes and situational factors of language

The other aspect not covered by the Bradford checklist concerns that part of language which may be referred to as the 'Why' and the 'When/Where'. This is also difficult to categorise and list though a few attempts are now being made in the literature to do so. It concerns the purposes for which language is used and the factors of situations which affect language. Would that we could see the rules here as clearly as we can see the grammatical rules. The former would be as much a part of the basic code as the latter.

The best thing we can do at this stage is to think very hard about the needs of our particular learners and to try to provide them with as appropriate a range of experiences as possible, noting the kinds of language which this demands. To some extent we have covered this already. For instance when we looked at the process of developing thought in the discussion about the five 'tions', we saw how certain language was needed for each step. This *language to match the steps of concept development* is one very important purpose for the young children with whom we are concerned.

Again the list of 'Categories of Experience' at the end of the Bradford checklist suggests another important purpose, *language to meet the needs of increasing knowledge of the world about them*. Each of these topics demands its own vocabulary and formulae. The list of 'Basic Sentence Types' shows another purpose. It is necessary for the learner to be able *to make statements, to describe and explain*, and it is necessary for him to be able *to ask questions* in order to find out information. It is also necessary for him to know how *to interact with others*, to respond to what others say and to carry on a conversation with one or more people. Then there is the need for *language to control others*, not only the form of instructions, requests or commands but more subtle things as well, such as persuasion and pleading etc. Note how important to these is the ability to use appropriate stress and intonation. Do we really make sure that we are covering all these things sufficiently with our second-language learners? The young child needs to learn these just as much as he needs the labels for the things he is handling in play if he is to become a fluent user of the second language.

Finally the child needs *ways of expressing his feelings*, again not only the words and groupings of words but also the appropriate sound features. And this leads on to something which has not as yet been covered and that is the need for *the language of make-believe*. Indeed it is through imaginative play that much of this work on the purposes of language is done. The child plays roles and sees himself in the other

54

person's shoes. He learns to feel with others as well as for himself and this the young child can do probably much more successfully than the older learner as he usually has fewer inhibitions. Teachers should make full use of this factor.

Make-believe play has in itself its own kind of language, things like 'Let's pretend' and 'You be the fairy'. Stories too have their language. Think how many fairy-tales start with the formula, 'Once upon a time' and end with 'They all lived happily ever after'. An analysis of fairy stories from this point of view would be worth while.

If we move on now from the 'Why' to the 'When' and 'Where' of language we find that *the social situation can also demand very specific kinds of language.* Sitting in the relaxed atmosphere of one's own home with a few intimate friends one would use very different language from that used at a formal staff meeting, for instance, or trapped in a burning building one's request for help would be in a very different style from that used in a shop when one wanted the shopkeeper's assistance. There are *many degrees of emotion, urgency and formality* to cope with depending on the interaction of such factors as time, place and people in the situation. Perhaps the words 'With Whom' should be added to When/Where.

But the teacher of young children must think about the particular situations in which her pupils have to use their second language. For a start we know that *they have to speak it in school.* Can we perhaps pick out some differences of situation here? There is the 'loose' chatting language of the field and there is the more controlled, specific language of the focus periods, and within these there is language used to the teacher and other adults and that used to other children. In addition there is *the language of the learning topic itself.*

Another range of situations where the child would have to use the second language is *in his dealings with people* such as policemen, street crossing attendants, nurses and doctors, etc. He may also have *to ask some other adult* to take him across a busy street, or to help him find his way home or to find his mother in a busy store. All of these situations suggest specific language and styles of language and a little thought on the part of the teacher could produce a list which could be included in the general checklist, and how helpful this would be as a source of ideas for role-play. Along with the personal purpose element, the social factors of language are just as important as the grammatical accuracy and they have their underlying rules too which are a part of the fluent speaker's code. So far as we can we must help our learners to acquire them. What has been given in this last section is not so much an inventory of language items as an attempt to highlight the areas which might produce such items. It is hoped that teachers will try to use it in this way.

Conclusion

The language checklist presented in this chapter emerged originally from the focusing of teachers on two areas of the school curriculum. This list, along with the sections on the sounds of English and the purposes and social factors, is intended only as a guide or framework within which to work. It may be, and it is certainly hoped, that one day a really comprehensive checklist will be produced by and for teachers of young children which will be the essential core of the language the young beginner must have in order to break through to fluency. This chapter is really at the heart of the book. It will be much referred to in the practical chapters which follow.

Further Reading

Aickman, D. *Rhymes for Speech and Action* University of London Press 1960

Dakin, J. *Songs and Rhymes for the Teaching of English* Longman 1968

French, F. G. *English in Tables* Oxford University Press 1960

Garvie, E. M. (ed.) *Language for the Foundations of Reading and Mathematics* City of Bradford Metropolitan Council Directorate of Educational Services, Spring 1974

Hornby, A. S. *The Teaching of Structural Words and Sentence Patterns Stage 1* Oxford University Press 1959

Pring, J. T. *Colloquial English Pronunciation* Longmans 1959

Robinson, W. P. and Rackstraw, S. J. *A Question of Answers* (Vols. 1 and 2) in the series, *Primary Socialisation, Language and Education,* ed. B. Bernstein, University of London, Institute of Education Sociological Research Unit 1972

Rudd, E. *Pronunciation for Non-English Speaking Children From India, Pakistan, Cyprus and Italy* Scope Handbook 2, Longman 1971

Quirk, R. *The Use of English* Longman 1962

Also

Scope Stage 1: An Introductory English Course for Immigrant Children Longman Books for Schools 1969

4
The Language 'Kit-bag'

Introduction

A helpful piece of equipment for small-group focusing sessions in the quiet room, especially in the Initial orientation period and the early stages of the next, is the language 'kit-bag'. It is helpful for the teacher as well as for the children because it assists her to focus on language for herself. It is simply a collection of objects selected mainly for their usefulness in highlighting the basic categories of experience, things such as colour, size and shape. Emphasis has already been given to the importance of what have been called the 'tions' and the language 'kit-bag' is designed to cater in particular for the first three, Identification, Qualification and Relation.

Whether or not an actual bag is used, is immaterial. The collection of objects can be kept anywhere which is convenient, but a portable kit has many advantages and a large bag made of some durable stuff such as canvas, is particularly useful. As to what it should contain, the following is only a suggestion but it is one which has been found useful in practice.

1. *Sets of:* balls, pencils and toy cars of different colours, sizes and shapes
2. *A set of:* bricks of different colours, sizes and shapes
3. *Some pieces of:* materials of different colours, textures and shapes
4. *An empty container*, e.g. a tin or box
5. *Another container* for keeping examples of familiar everyday objects, e.g. comb, key, purse, coin etc.

Most of this material, once it has been thoughtfully selected, should remain as a permanent kit so that the familiar can be used to teach other things, but the objects at number 5 should be changed as the children become able to label them. In other words once the objects in 1–4 are known and can be named, they are used to teach and to keep on practising the language of colour, shape, size, texture, etc., along with that of simple relationships. They are also used for focusing on structure and practising sentence patterns.

The use of the 'kit-bag'

It will be remembered that the aim of this focusing work is to slow down and concentrate on certain aspects of the learning field so that the children have a chance to consolidate their learning and so that any difficulties can be cleared away. It should be a very deliberate matching of experience and language. The children have to learn to look and listen as well as to speak. Though the 'kit-bag' can be used for focusing with the individual child it is probably most useful in group-work. Here are a few general points to bear in mind.

(a) *Situation*

1. It is advisable to have a reasonably quiet corner or room set apart for this work and there should be at least one other adult/fluent speaker helping the teacher.

2. The children should be seated on the floor in a semi-circle with the 'presenting' teacher sitting on a low chair in front and the helper(s) sitting with the children. All should be able to see the presenter clearly.

3. The materials from the 'kit-bag' to be used should all be at hand and arranged in order of presentation, and if additional apparatus is needed such as pieces of furniture or other things too large for the 'bag', then these should be ready at the side.

4. No session should last very long. It is up to the presenter to judge the situation. Five to ten minutes in the early stages is quite adequate, but if the work is lively and interesting it might last twenty.

5. At the end of the session the contents of the 'bag' should be replaced and left ready for the next time. It may seem unnecessary to say this but

in the business of organising the children it is all too easy for equipment to be pushed somewhat haphazardly away so that valuable time is lost when it comes to be used again. Either the presenter herself or one of the helpers should take responsibility for returning the materials to their 'rest' position.

(b) *Presentation*

1. The presenter must make the underlying meaning as clear as possible, using not only her 'kit' but also appropriate actions and facial expressions.

2. The language 'model' must be one of careful enunciation, with due consideration to matters of pronunciation, stress and intonation.

3. Careful timing is essential. The presenter must judge just when to give the words which match the experience. It often pays to linger over the visual presentation before any words are spoken at all. Teachers should not be afraid of meaningful silence.

4. Opportunities must be given for listening and looking and for imitation and practice.

5. The presenter should make as much use of the other helpers in the situation as she needs, particularly in the early stages. They are there to help show the children how to interpret instructions as well as to show how things should be said.

Let us go on now to some illustration of the 'kit-bag' being used, starting with the complete beginner.

The Beginner

The aim is to be sure that he can recognise and label a few objects and that he has at least one structure for 'slotting' the names of the objects into, for example:

Stimulus		Response	
Action	*Language*	*Action*	*Language*
Presenter picks up the ball and shows it to the group.	This is a ball. a ball ball This is a ball.		
Presenter gives the ball to a helper.	You say it.	Helper shows the ball to the children.	This is a ball. a ball ball This is a ball.

If there is more than one helper the procedure can again be repeated. Then the children are encouraged to take part. Teacher and helpers can each stand with a child, putting their hands round the child's hands as he clutches the ball and saying the sentence with him until he has the confidence to say it on his own. The reason for breaking down the structure into 'a ball' and 'ball' is that a learner must be helped to see which part of the series of noises really attaches to the object. As far as he knows the name of the object could be 'this'. Eventually of course after he has heard 'This is a ——' with a great many objects, it would become clear that 'this' is not an object name, and the breaking down of the structure would no longer be necessary.

It might take several focusing sessions before all the children in a group have understood sufficiently and have enough confidence to pick up the ball, pencil, etc., and make the statement, but this is what the teacher should be aiming towards. The children should be able to recognise and to label all the objects in the 'kit-bag', with those in the inner container being changed when their names have been learnt, as we saw above.

Further work

Here now is a plan for several focusing sessions at a later stage. How much is done in any one session depends on the particular circumstances. It is assumed that the work has covered the plural and qualification by colour and size. The aims here are as follows:

1. To revise the name of the object, 'ball' and the colour words, 'red', 'blue' and 'yellow'.

2. To revise the plural.

3. To revise the size words, 'big' and 'small'.

4. To focus for the first time on the new words
                          'bigger' and 'biggest'
                          'smaller' and 'smallest'

MATERIALS:

sets of coloured balls, three in each set, red, blue and yellow.
a small, middle-sized and big ball in each set.

LANGUAGE TO BE COVERED

(i.e. that the child should be able to say):

Structure	*Vocabulary*
This is a ——.	ball, balls
It's a ——.	red, blue, yellow
It's a (adj.) (noun).	big, small
These are ——s.	bigger, smaller
They are ——s.	biggest, smallest
——er than ——	
—— the ——est	

PROCEDURE:

Stimulus		Response	
Action	*Language*	*Action*	*Language*
Presenter picks up a ball	This is a ball.		
Gives ball to child	You say it.	Child holding ball	This is a ball.
Presenter with the same ball back	What's this?	Group together	It's a ball.
Presenter repeats but to one child	What's this?	Child alone	It's a ball.
Presenter lays out a ball of the same size from each set and first picks up the red one.	What colour is this ball?	Group together	It's a red ball.
Presenter repeats but to one child	What colour is this ball?	Child alone	It's a red ball.

(Sequence is repeated with blue and yellow)

62

Stimulus		Response	
Action	*Language*	*Action*	*Language*
Presenter picks up two balls of different colours	These are balls		
Gives them to a child	You say it.	Child holding balls	These are balls.
Presenter with the same balls back.	What are these?	Group together	They are balls.
Presenter repeats but to one child	What are these?	Child alone	They are balls.

(The colour sequence should now be repeated with the plural, e.g. 'What colour are these balls? They are red balls'.)

Presenter holds the biggest ball of a set in one hand and the smallest in the other	This ball is big. This ball is small. (Care with stress and intonation to suggest contrast)		
Gives balls to helper	You say it.	Helper holding balls	This ball is big. This ball is small.
Helper gives balls to a child	You say it.	Child holding balls	This ball is big. This ball is small.
Presenter lays out the three balls of one of the sets in order of size then touches appropriate balls	This ball is bigger than this ball. This ball is bigger than this ball.		
Says to helper	You say it.	Helper touching the appropriate balls	This ball is bigger than this ball. This ball is bigger than this ball.

(If there is more than one helper, each should be asked to do this and then each should take a child and ask him/her to repeat. The presenter should then ask one child to do it for the group. Then the whole sequence should be repeated with the balls being touched in the opposite direction so that 'smaller' and 'smallest' can be covered.)

Presenter again with one set of balls, touches the middle one then the smallest then the biggest	This ball is bigger than this ball. This ball is the biggest.		

Stimulus		Response	
Action	*Language*	*Action*	*Language*
(This is repeated with all three sets.)			
Presenter to helper (each in turn if more than one) with each set	Show me the biggest ball.	Helper touches it.	
(This is repeated with children.)			
Presenter again	This ball is bigger than this ball. This ball is the biggest.		
Presenter to helpers and then to children	You say it.	Helpers and then children individually touching the appropriate balls	This ball is bigger than this ball. This ball is the biggest.

(The whole sequence should be repeated with appropriate movements to show 'smallest', and then repetition of all this could be done to bring in the colour names again, e.g. 'This red ball is bigger than this red ball', etc.)

Both the language and the procedure are only suggestions. It is possible to bring in all kinds of variations and the order of their presentation is by no means rigid. But teachers must be sure that they are covering the checklist. Other items around this stage are, for example, the nearness/farness distinction, 'this/that' and 'these/those' where the appropriate actions would be touching for the first and pointing for the second, the negative as in 'This is not a ball', and the use of 'one' as in 'red one'.

In addition the children themselves should be taught to ask as well as to answer the questions. They have to learn to use all the basic sentence types and here they could learn to say, 'What's this?', 'What are these?' and 'What colour is the ———?' with teachers, helpers and other children answering. At first the helpers would have to demonstrate what was required, as is illustrated for other things in the above sequences. The children should also be encouraged to give instructions such as, 'Show me the biggest ball', etc.

With the reluctant speaker

The 'kit-bag' is useful when working with children who show little motivation to speak at all. Most teachers are familiar with the child who appears to understand quite a lot, who carries out simple instructions quite cheerfully, but who seldom if ever makes any communication except perhaps to nod or shake his head. How can the teacher encourage these 'nodders' to speak? Here is an idea which has worked with some. It might be worth developing.

The group of children should be quite small, perhaps about six in all. The teacher should sit or kneel on the floor with them, clutching her bag of objects, and to begin with she should say nothing at all. All the communication is done by action. First she opens the bag very slowly with little peeps inside and expectant looks at the children, then she pulls something out and holds it for all to see before placing it on the floor. Gradually the floor is covered with a mixture of objects from the bag, some of which match and some of which do not.

Still without speaking the teacher should put the bag away from her and concentrate now on the objects on the floor. After pretending to think hard she selects one, for example a long blue brick, and holds this up for all to see. She then looks round again and picks up a long yellow one. Holding these together she lets it be seen that she has made a mistake, that this is not what she really wanted. She should shake her head and look suitably displeased and she should put the yellow brick back again. Her eye then catches another blue brick and with great joy she picks this up and holds it with the original blue one. But unfortunately the second one is shorter. Once again she is displeased and replaces the short blue brick. Finally she spots another blue brick which, when held up with the first, is seen to be the same in all respects. Great triumph must be demonstrated and the two bricks laid reverently to one side!

The same procedure should then be gone through again, and perhaps a third time with another brick or with another object. The chances are that by the time the third or even the second sequence is in operation, the children are beginning to come to life. If the work is done well, with lots of clear actions and facial expressions, the children learn very soon what is supposed to be happening and they become almost desperate when the teacher cannot see the matching object. Sometimes one child will tug the teacher's sleeve and point to the object. Sometimes a child will grunt and point. But best of all a child will occasionally burst into speech. It may only be something like, 'Teacher here', but it is a big step forward.

The child who spoke should receive a tremendous ovation with the teacher now also speaking for the first time and saying something like, 'Good boy/girl'. This should be quickly followed by a helper expanding what the child said into, for example, 'Teacher, it's here', and the presenter responding with something like, 'Yes, it's here'. She should then pick up the matching objects and say, 'These two are the same'. The whole thing should be repeated as long as the interest holds.

In the writer's experience the first words of any kind spoken by a child in the group constitute a breakthrough. If they are received with appropriate approval and carefully followed up, not only is this usually the beginning of oracy for the child in question, but it often is also for others in the group. The word 'same' in this example leads on to the word 'different' and the children in the group begin to mutter these words under their breath. Eventually the muttering becomes louder and more confident, and complete structures which have possibly been understood but remained passive, begin now to be spoken. There is nothing quite so worthwhile for the hard-pressed teacher than this kind of reward for patient work. The technique highlights the importance of ensuring meaning, motivation and interest and then supplying the appropriate means of expression.

Some games with the objects

It was suggested that in the language 'kit-bag' there should be a collection of familiar objects for the children to identify and label, kept together in another bag or container of some kind. This 'guessing-bag' can be used in different ways. Here are one or two ideas:

1. *A simple guessing game*

For children with very little English who have learnt to respond to the question, 'What's this?':

Stimulus		Response	
Action	*Language*	*Action*	*Language*
Presenter to a helper as she (the presenter) dips her hand in the bag and clutches an object	What's this? Guess.	Helper, thinking hard, and deliberately saying the wrong thing	It's a ball.
Presenter bringing out a comb.	No it isn't. It's a comb.		

This is repeated with different objects, sometimes the 'guess' being correct and sometimes wrong. If the helper is right the presenter says, 'Yes it is. It's a ———'. Then the children begin to take part, eventually also acting as the one with the bag and the one in the group who guesses right is given the bag the next time.

2. *The attributes game*

For children with a little more English who have learnt some words for qualification here is another guessing game. Again the presenter and helpers go through the procedure first. The guesser is blindfolded and the presenter when she picks something out of the bag says something such as the following as she shows the object to the rest of the group:

This is blue. It's long. It's hard. It's made of wood', etc. What is it?

The child responds in the same way as for the last game:

It's a ———', and the presenter says, 'Yes, it is', or 'No, it isn't. Try again.'

3. *A simple dialogue*

This is for children at all levels. The language can be very simple to start with and it can be elaborated gradually. The objects from the 'guessing-bag' and those in the rest of the language 'kit-bag' are spread out on a table. The children are taught in the same way as before, that is by helpers acting and speaking first.

Presenter	What do you want?
Child	May I have a ———, please?
Presenter	Yes, here you are.
Child	Thank you.

Eventually a child will take the part of the presenter.
Varieties can be introduced as follows:

(a) *A little extension*

Presenter	What do you want now?
Child	May I have another ——, please?
Presenter	What colour do you want?
Child	May I have the green one, please?
Presenter	Yes, here you are. Here's the green one.
Child	Thank you.

(b) *More elaboration*

Presenter	What would you like today?
Child	May I have two ——s and three ——s, please?
Presenter	Do you want long ——s or short ones?
Child	I want short ones, please.
Presenter	And do you want red ones or blue ones?
Child	I want blue ones, please.
Presenter	Here you are. Here are two short blue ——s.
	Now, do you want hard ——s or soft ones?
Child	I want soft ones, please.
Presenter	And do you want ——s with paper on or ——s without paper on?
Child	I want ——s with paper on, please.
Presenter	Here you are. Here are three soft ——s with paper on.
Child	Thank you.

It can be seen that all kinds of interesting extensions can be introduced. Again teachers should refer to the checklist for ideas of language to cover. The children should be given the opportunity to play both parts in the dialogues. Work of this kind can be done on a much wider scale in large group focusing or community happenings, as we shall see in the next chapter, but here in the small group with the use of objects from the 'kit-bag', some very useful practice at depth can be done with all the children in the group taking part.

Practising the prepositions

Here the empty tin or box can be used and a few of the objects from the 'kit-bag'. The first simple step might be as follows:

Stimulus		Response	
Action	*Language*	*Action*	*Language*
Presenter showing the box	What's this?	Group together	It's a box.
Presenter to a helper	Put the comb in the box.	Helper does so	
Presenter	Where is the comb?	Helper, pointing to the comb	It's in the box.

After a number of the prepositions have been practised in this way with various familiar objects being used, the whole thing can be turned into a game. Possibly two boxes could be used, one for each of two teams, and points would be gained for the fastest correct responses to instructions such as:

Put the comb under the box.
Put the yellow pencil in the box, etc.

The prepositions *do* need to be practised a great deal as this is one area of language where there can be much 'interference' of learning. For instance, as we have seen the Punjabi word for 'in' sounds very much like the English word 'under'. Teachers should beware of presenting English 'in' and 'under' together in the early stages. Also within English itself, the sounds of 'under' and 'on the' are very similar. Again it would be wise not to present these two together at first.

An important technical point is that care must be taken in practice to see that the relationship being illustrated is the same for all. Depending on where people are, an object can be 'in front of' for some and 'behind' for others. All these things are vital learning factors and it is worth spending time and thought on them.

Conclusion

There are a great many other techniques which could be illustrated here but perhaps enough has been covered to give an idea of the potential usefulness of the language 'kit-bag'. It must be remembered that the equipment is meant for the very early stages of language work and that it is as much a point of focus for the teacher as for the children. Of course the same kind of things can be done with other objects in the field and it is hoped that they will be, but the risk is that the work can be rather haphazard if the teacher does not collect her ideas in one place. Probably the easiest way to do this is to attach them to one set of equipment in the beginning. As the children move on in the second phase both they and the teacher are better able to tackle the widening field of infant school work, building on the basic language acquired by means of focusing on the more limited field represented by the work suggested in this chapter. The language 'kit-bag' is as much a way of thinking for the teacher as an actual piece of equipment. It becomes eventually the entire curriculum.

Further Reading

Garvie, E. M. 'The Language "Kit-bag"' in *Under Fives and Community Relations* Vol. 1; No. 3, July 1975

5
The Community Happening

Introduction

The community happening is the name being given here to the large-group activity concerned with role-play. It is seen as a particularly valuable technique for focusing on the social concepts and the functions and situational appropriateness of language. Whilst it is recognised that similar work can be done in smaller groups, it is suggested that the community activity has certain particular advantages which are perhaps too often overlooked. One of these is the wide scope which is offered for variety of approach. The greater numbers of people to draw on and the tremendous sense of togetherness make the planning and the procedure in some ways easier and in every way exciting.

It has been said earlier that community activities are specially valuable at the Initial orientation stage and that role-play or happenings are useful for making clear to the bewildered beginner some of the new experiences of school which he is meeting for the first time, particularly in the area of social relationships. An attempt will be made to try to illustrate this. The community happening can also be used, perhaps with less frequency, at the later stages and examples will also be given of this, bearing in mind the increasing language fluency in general, the growth in thought development and the increasing ability of the child to initiate his own ploys. But first some points about the community happening in general; the planning, the deployment of personnel, and the procedure.

General points

(a) As in all this work the teachers must plan together as a team. They should be aware of the particular needs of the group of children

71

concerned and begin by listing ideas which would be possible for role-plays before selecting the most useful for detailed planning.

(b) To be really successful the happening should have at least four leading adults, two or more to act, one to monitor and one to lead the 'chorus'. In addition there could be many other adults mingling with the children. Other teachers, non-teaching staff, older English-speaking children and students, and the parents of the children, could all help to augment the teaching team, provided that the latter knows what it is doing. It could be in fact that this real community happening might be a valuable experience for parents from other cultures, and if there were home–liaison workers on the staff they could encourage the parents to come. Indeed the parents and home–liaison workers might well be able to offer useful ideas for role-plays.

(c) It is important that the acting area should be clearly seen by everybody in the room. The arrangements for acting and the seating of the participating audience must be carefully worked out. It is useful also if there is a permanent properties corner with easy access to the acting area. Mention has been made of this before in connection with the visual aids for singing. Many of these same things can be used in role-play.

(d) There is no suggestion of staging a play with elaborate scenery and costume. Time does not permit this and it is doubtful in any case if sophisticated drama would serve the purpose of the community happening. All that is required is the suggestion of the appropriate scene and characters by the imaginative use of such things as the home-corner or shop, ordinary tables and chairs and different hats etc. from the dressing-up collection. Teachers will soon begin to discover the things which are most useful and these can always be kept ready.

(e) The most important person in the happening is the monitor. It is she who really takes control and acts as mistress of ceremonies. She is the leader of the team. Even at the planning stage someone has to be 'in the chair' and it is useful if this is also the person who is going to monitor the proceedings for the children. It could be the Head or it could be a teacher who has made it her special responsibility, perhaps working with the parents and home–liaison workers, to study the things which

72

bewilder and cause particular difficulties and perhaps even to record them as an addition to the school *language* checklist.

From her knowledge of these and the use of the language checklist in general, the monitor guides her colleagues to provide helpful happenings with particular emphases, sometimes conceptual, sometimes linguistic, though always of course there must be a careful matching of concept and language. During the proceedings she can increase or decrease the amount of monitoring as she sees fit. She must also control the pace of events and, perhaps most difficult of all, she must be prepared to cope with the unexpected, the actress who 'does it wrong', the member of the 'chorus' who says the wrong thing, the interruption from outside etc. All of these incidents can in fact be put to good use by the monitor who is alert and skilled.

(f) The other adults also have important parts to play. The two or more who do the acting must really understand what they are trying to get across. The team as a whole, guided by the monitor, will have decided what this is. The performers are responsible for putting the purposes of the team into action and each role-play should be adequately rehearsed in a general way, allowing for the spontaneous element of the real happening.

It is the task of the 'chorus' leader, assisted by the other helpers, sitting amongst the children, to encourage responses from the latter. The whole effect should be rather like a theatre during a children's pantomime, with the monitor behaving in the manner of the comedian who comments on the scene and puts questions and instructions to the audience, the 'chorus' leader in the role of the comedian's stooge who has gone into the audience, and the other helpers taking the parts of the fond parents who encourage their offspring to take part in the proceedings. The happening should try to catch the interest, generate some excitement and in general be a highly motivating experience.

(g) Finally it is helpful for the teaching team to keep a record of the community happenings. Tape-recordings might even be attempted, though success with these in large groups demands considerable expertise and the use of fairly sophisticated apparatus. This is where the co-operation of college staff might be sought. In return for the help with recording, the college could have the use of the tapes as training material. But even a written record of the plans of the role-plays, along with some notes on how they worked in practice, would be useful for future reference.

A possible 'Community Happening'

At the Initial orientation stage one part of the school day which is sometimes very bewildering for children is dinner-time. The whole procedure from hand-washing in the cloakroom to queuing for the courses, to eating, sometimes with unaccustomed utensils, to going for second helpings, to bringing back the empty dishes with plates in one place and cutlery in another, etc., can cause considerable confusion and unhappiness for many children in the beginning. Some slowing down of the 'film' with focusing on the significant parts of the routine, might make the subject of a useful happening. Here is a possible presentation. It has to be remembered that this is a very general plan which will alter with circumstances. The plan is divided into three mini-happenings each of which could be developed and extended into a fuller happening on its own.

1. THE PLAYGROUND

Two 'children' are playing with balls in the playground.

'Teacher' (clapping her hands)
    It's dinner-time.
    Come and wash your hands.
    (with gestures)
    Put your balls down.
    Come and wash your hands.

The 'children' do so and follow the 'teacher'. All three actresses go to the side and keep still or they go behind a screen if this is possible. The monitor takes over.

Monitor (looking about her)
    Oh, they've gone.
    Where have they gone?
    Are they here?
    No, they're not here.
    Are they over there?
Chorus (with help of leader)
    No, they're not here, etc.

Meantime the actresses appear again. They face the community and pretend to turn on taps and wash their hands. The 'teacher' stands at the side.

74

2. THE CLOAKROOM

Monitor (with her back to the actresses)
Where are they?
Are they in the playground?

Chorus   No, they're not.
Leader   Look. They are in the cloakroom.
Monitor   No, they're not.
Chorus   Yes, they are, etc.
Monitor   What are they doing?
Chorus   They are washing their hands. Look.

The monitor turns and watches the actresses and all eyes and ears are now directed there.

'Teacher'   Turn on the taps.
This is the hot tap.

The 'children' act with suitable reaction to the hot water.

Monitor   What's that?
Leader   It's the hot tap.
'Teacher'   This is the cold tap.
Monitor   What's that?
Chorus   It's the cold tap.
'Teacher'   This is the plug.
Put the plug in.
Monitor   What's that?
Chorus   It's the plug.
'Teacher'   This is the soap.
Monitor   What's that?
Chorus   It's the soap.
'Teacher'   Wash your hands.

The 'children' do so.

Monitor   What are they doing?
Chorus   They're washing their hands.
Monitor   Are they playing?
Chorus   No, they're not.
Monitor   What are they doing?
Chorus   They're washing their hands.

                  etc.

This can be extended at the monitor's discretion. The 'argument' technique is very useful as it helps to practise the short forms such as, 'Yes, they are' and 'No, they aren't'. The action would then proceed to the use of the towel and the business of drying the hands, which could be treated in the same manner.

At this stage the actresses again leave the scene and an interlude such as the following might be attempted:

Monitor	Let's wash our hands.
	Turn on the hot tap.
	Turn on the cold tap.
	Put the plug in.
	Take the soap.
	Wash your hands.

Helped by the adults around them all the real children pretend to do these actions.

Monitor	What are you doing?
Chorus	We're washing our hands.
Monitor	Are you playing?
Chorus	No, we're not.
Monitor (to leader)	
	Are they playing?
Leader	No, they're not.
	They're washing their hands.

This can be repeated with the business of drying the hands, at the end of which the actresses reappear. A table and chairs have been placed for them.

3. THE DINING-ROOM

Monitor	Oh, here they are again.
	What are they going to do now?
	Are they going to play?
Leader	No, they're not.
Monitor	Are they going to wash their hands?
Leader	No, they're not.
Monitor	What are they going to do?
Leader	They're going to have dinner.

This should be repeated with the chorus answering along with the leader.

Monitor	Let's watch them.

The use of cutlery is perhaps the most difficult problem of this particular experience for many children. Again the action and monitoring should be planned accordingly with appropriate focusing on the names of the utensils, their particular functions, and the hands used for each. The following is a possibility:

All eyes are on the acting area.

'Teacher'	Show me your right hand.

'Children' do so. The actresses hold their positions.

Monitor (to the chorus)	Show me your right hand.

The real children do so with help from the adults.

The same business is repeated with the left hand, first the actresses doing it, then the community at large.

'Teacher' (picking up a knife)
   Put your knife in your right hand.

The 'children' do so.

'Teacher' (picking up a fork)
   Put your fork in your left hand.

The 'children' do so. The 'teacher' holds up a knife for all to see.

Monitor	What's that?
Chorus	It's a knife.

The 'teacher' holds up a fork for all to see.

Monitor	What's that?
Chorus	It's a fork.
Monitor	Is it a towel?
Chorus	No, it isn't.
Monitor	Is it a knife?
Chorus	No, it isn't.
Monitor	What is it?
Chorus	It's a fork.

Monitor (as 'children' eat)
   Look. They are having dinner.

 The business of eating should go on for a few seconds, possibly with the 'children' having some difficulty with the cutlery. Then:

'Teacher' Put your fork like this.
   Cut with your knife.

The 'children' use the cutlery properly.

Monitor Let's all do it.
   Put your fork like this.
   Cut with your knife.

The adults help the real children to pretend.

'Teacher' Eat your dinner.
   Put your fork in your mouth.

The 'children' do so.

Monitor Let's all do it.
   Eat your dinner.
   Put your fork in your mouth.
          etc.

 This could be extended to cover deliberate mistakes made by the 'children' with the 'teacher' correcting. If done skilfully the 'audience' enjoys seeing their teachers make

77

mistakes and the whole proceedings can be fun. But again the language must be carefully controlled and it must match the experience very closely.

The action could then go on to demonstrate second helpings, the pudding course and the use of a spoon, and the clearing away of plates and cutlery. The use of water glasses might also be included.

Perhaps enough has now been illustrated to give the idea of a community happening at the Initial orientation stage. It is not suggested that all of this be done in one happening. The teaching team must decide how much they think the children can take and how detailed it can be. The same framework could be used more than once with variety of content and action.

Other topics for the Initial orientation stage

Some other suggestions for themes which could be used at this very early stage follow. The detailed working out is left for teaching teams to do for themselves.

(a) *Milk-time followed by playtime*

Naturally each school should work according to its own routine but many do have a pause for drinking milk after which the children go into the playground. Milk-time is generally less complicated than dinner-time but it cannot be assumed that children will know immediately what to do without help, nor that they will 'pick up' the language of the procedure simply by being exposed to it daily. Again ideas for knowing what to do with playtime have often to be given. Most teachers are familiar with the children who stand in a corner looking on, with a mixture of longing and bewilderment, while other children play. They are just not used to occupying themselves in this way and the leadership of the other children is not enough to set them going. A community happening which demonstrates the use of a limited number of playthings such as balls and ropes, can be a help. Certain running and hiding games might also be introduced in this way. But more imaginative games would be more difficult because of the limited language which can be used at this stage.

(b) *Coming to school and going home*

Again procedures differ from school to school. The children may walk or have a journey by vehicle. Road safety could come in here and crossing with the help of the crossing man/lady. It may even be possible to bring the real crossing man/lady into the school for the community happening. Procedure in the cloakroom could be covered and things like collection of dinner money and the business of other things the children have to carry from time to time, such as notes home to mother.

(c) *Visit of the school dentist/doctor/nurse, etc.*

An added advantage of doing a community happening around this theme is that it could remove some of the apprehension which many children experience during such visits. For the children to see their teachers submitting to the same treatment and a kind of game being made of the whole thing, is fun and reassuring. Special gimmicks such as the 'dentist' down on his knees hunting for the lost tooth which eventually turns up in an odd place, can give further interest and enjoyment.

(d) *A school outing*

Most teaching teams plan such an event so that it not only gives pleasure at the time but that it also forms part of the general learning procedure. It has to be prepared for and followed up. One of the follow-up activities could be a community happening, with teachers acting out the event or at least some part of it. This is particularly valuable for the once-only experience, as it will help the children to remember the details and not only a vague overall impression. Unlike school routines which are regularly practised and consolidated, these outside events are fleeting and can be quickly forgotten especially if there is little support from the home background.

Before we move on now to suggestions for community happenings at later stages, it must be stressed that one of the aims in all this work is to try to involve all the children as much as possible. This is one of the main values of the chorus responses. But also, after several

79

'performances' of a happening a few of the more fluent and confident children could begin to take the parts which the teachers had enacted, while the adults go on to plan and perform more elaborate happenings.

One would hope, in addition, that the children's 'free' play might begin to reflect the community happenings, and the teachers in their general supervision should encourage this. We have all experienced at some time the amusing 'take-off' of ourselves as teachers which can happen in the classroom. Very often the child concerned is quite unconscious of what he/she is doing. In a situation where the teachers are deliberately performing for the children this might happen more often and it could be very useful language practice.

Suggestions for the Cracking the code stage

It will be remembered that at this second stage all the activities of the first school curriculum are introduced, albeit in a limited way to start with. The children have learnt to cope with the initial bewilderment of school and certain 'survival language' is within their power.

They are now ready for learning the things which particular classroom activities offer. Here then is the source of material for further community happenings.

Perhaps the most obvious example is the story, action song or rhyme. Teachers could very easily develop these into useful community happenings with the help of other adults. This is in fact what happens in a real theatre pantomime when the comedian brings the audience into the proceedings. Sometimes he enlists their help such as asking them to boo or hiss when the villain appears, or to keep the secret of where he has hidden the princess etc. So much useful language work could be done by careful planning of things like this.

What is perhaps less obvious is the usefulness of role-plays connected with play at the water-tank, sand-tray or building blocks, etc. The aim here would be to focus upon and perhaps to extend the activities which the children had discovered for themselves, with the addition of the appropriate verbal element. Teachers should bear in mind in particular the first three 'tions', Identification, Qualification and Relation, and try to 'peg' the language accordingly. Here now are two happenings, one to illustrate the use of a story and the other the use of building blocks.

1. The story

In Donn Byrne's Picture Compositions (see references) the first story is about a little girl who is playing with a ball when a dog runs off with it. All is well, however, when her father comes to comfort her and retrieves the ball. There are three characters, the girl, the dog and the father. Here is a plan for a community happening around this theme.

At the beginning the girl is bouncing the ball and the dog is barking hopefully.

Girl	This is *my* ball.
	It's not *your* ball.
	Go away.

The girl drops the ball which rolls out of sight. (This would take some practice!) The dog goes out after it barking.

Girl (crying)	The dog's got my ball.
	The dog's got my ball.
	Come back. Come back.
	I want my ball.

She goes out crying.

Monitor	Why is she crying?
	What's the matter?
Chorus Leader	She's lost her ball.
Monitor	Has she lost her money?
Chorus	No, she hasn't.
Monitor	Has she lost her shoe?
Chorus	No, she hasn't.
Monitor	What has she lost?
Chorus	She's lost her ball.
Chorus Leader	The dog's got her ball.
Monitor	Tell me again. I can't hear you.
Chorus	The dog's got her ball.
Monitor	Why is she crying?
Chorus	The dog's got her ball.
Monitor	Tell me again.
Chorus	The dog's got her ball.

The girl comes back, still crying.

Girl	I want my ball. I want my ball.
Father	Why are you crying?
	What's the matter?
Girl	The dog's got my ball.
	I want my ball.
Father	Don't cry. I'll get your ball.
	Come with me.

They go out and the dog is heard barking.

Monitor	Where have they gone?
Chorus Leader	They've gone to get the ball.
Monitor	I can't hear you. Tell me again.
Chorus	They've gone to get the ball.
Monitor	Where is the ball?
Chorus Leader	The dog's got it.
Monitor	Has the cat got it?
Chorus	No, it hasn't
Monitor	Has the monkey got it?
Chorus	No, it hasn't.
Monitor	Where is the ball?
Chorus	The dog's got it.

The girl comes back holding her father's hand. She is smiling now.

Girl	Look. I've got my ball.
	I've got my ball.
	Daddy helped me.
	Thank you, Daddy.

The dog is heard barking and the father goes out saying:

Father	Go away. Go away.
	You naughty dog.

The girl goes out the other way, throwing her ball and catching it, in time with what she is saying.

Girl	I've got my ball.
	I've got my ball, etc.

Monitor and chorus take up the chant:

Monitor and Chorus	
	She's got her ball.
	She's got her ball, etc.

They could use clapping or arm movements of some kind.

2. Building blocks

Two 'children' are playing with the blocks.

'Child 1'	Let's build a house.
'Child 2'	This is the door.
'Child 1'	No, make the wall first.
'Child 2'	Here's a long block.
'Child 1'	Here's a longer one.
	This is better.
'Child 2'	Here are some more like that.
	Find some more.
'Child 1'	Here's another one.
	And here's another one.
	Let's put them like this.

The 'children' go on building quietly.

Monitor	What are they building?
Chorus Leader	They are building a house.
Monitor	They are building a shop.
Chorus	No, they aren't
Monitor	Yes, they are.
Chorus	No, they aren't
Monitor	What are they building?
Chorus	They are building a house.
Monitor	Are they making the door?
Chorus Leader	No, they are making the wall first.
Monitor	Tell me again. I can't hear you.
Chorus	They are making the wall first.
Monitor	Are they using short blocks?
Chorus Leader	No, they are using long ones.
Monitor	Are they very long blocks?
Chorus Leader	Ask us again. We can't hear you.
Monitor	Are they very long blocks?
Chorus	Yes, they are.
Monitor	Let me see.

She goes over to the 'children'.

Monitor	Oh yes. They are using very long blocks.
	They are making the wall.
	They are nearly finished.

This happening could then be extended to include descriptions of the building of other parts of the house, the same procedure being followed, that is, the 'children' chatting together first and then the monitor questioning and commenting. It is important to remember that at this stage the children must have lots of practice in (a) giving information (b) asking for information and (c) giving instructions. Examples of each of these in the above sequence are:

(a) giving information	They are making the wall first.
(b) asking for information	Are they very long blocks?
(c) giving an instruction	Find some more.

They also need practice in labelling, for example, 'house', 'door' and 'wall', in the use of qualifying words such as 'long' and 'short' and structures for showing relationship such as 'a longer one'.

Teachers should try to devise other happenings along the same lines with stories which *their* children enjoy and with activities in other areas of the curriculum. At this stage too the outside visits, etc., will continue, giving another source of material for community happenings which can now use language which is a little more complex.

Suggestions for the Breakthrough to fluency stage

Once the children have 'cracked the code' the aim is to help them to increase their fluency. The children themselves should take much more part in the role-plays, both in the planning and in the performing. One useful idea is to have them perform a role-play for the less fluent children. There is nothing like teaching others for helping one's own learning. But also even the better children will benefit by the occasional community happening which is specially planned to cater for their own increasing expertise.

Concerning the first idea, if the children are used to community happenings and have perhaps even taken acting parts in those devised by the teachers, they will know the procedure. Teachers and children together can then concentrate on the content. The children may wish at first to repeat the happenings they have already experienced and this is probably a good plan initially, but they should be encouraged to make some innovations of their own and to go on to producing ideas for completely new happenings. It could be that in the beginning a teacher should act as monitor, but even this part could eventually be taken by a child, giving him very useful practice in revising lots of language patterns, particularly the question forms.

For the more elaborate happening devised to stretch and challenge the more fluent children, the work should be aimed at ringing the changes on previous learning by showing, for instance, different and more complex ways of saying things. It should also be aimed at the development of imaginative thought with language which expresses events past, future and possible. The following examples illustrate these two notions.

1. *Ringing the changes on previous learning*

It might be useful not only to extend the language used previously but also to repeat a theme such as the story of the little girl and her ball which was described above. Here is an example of a more elaborate happening, showing how the language used at an early stage can be increased and made more complex. Again the characters are the little girl, her father and the dog. The scenes follow the same pattern as before so only the dialogues will be given. Note that it is probable at this stage that the chorus can do with much less adult help. The leader may well be one of the children, or there may be no leader at all.

Girl	You can't have my ball because I want to play with it.
	You mustn't take it, you naughty dog. Go away.
Girl	Oh, dear! The dog's taken my ball and I *did* want to play with it.
	What a naughty dog!
	I wish I had my ball back.
Monitor	What's the matter with the little girl?
Chorus Leader	The dog's stolen her ball and she wants to play with it.
Monitor	Has she had her purse stolen?
Chorus Leader	No, her ball.

Note the short, natural form of the last sentence. This should begin to happen at this stage. More will be said about it in the next chapter.

Monitor	Has someone taken her sweets?
Chorus Leader	No, the dog's taken her ball.
Monitor	Tell me again what happened.
Chorus	The dog's taken her ball.
Monitor	Speak up. I can't hear you.
Chorus	The dog's taken her ball.
Girl	I still haven't got my ball and I *do* want it.
Father	What's the trouble?
Girl	That naughty dog from next door has stolen my ball and I *do* want it back.
Father	Never mind. I'll get it back for you.
	Come along with me.
Monitor	Where are they off to?
Chorus Leader	To get the ball back.
Monitor	Pardon?
Chorus	To get the ball back.
Monitor	Where is it?
Chorus Leader	The dog has it. He wanted to play with it.
Monitor	Did you say the cat had it?
Chorus Leader	No, I didn't.
(to rest of chorus)	What *did* I say?
Chorus	You said the dog had it.
Monitor	Did she say the monkey had it?
Chorus	No, she didn't.
Monitor	What *did* she say then?
Chorus	She said the dog had it.

Monitor	Where is the ball?
Chorus	The dog has it.
Girl	Look. I've got my ball back again.
	Daddy helped me to get it. He took it out of the dog's mouth.
	Thank you for helping me, Daddy.
Father	You're a naughty dog. Off you go.
	The ball is not for you.

Girl (singing while she plays, to the tune of Round the Mulberry Bush)

> Now I'm happy I've got my ball,
> I've got my ball, I've got my ball.
> Now I'm happy I've got my ball,
> On a bright and sunny morning.

Community	Now she's happy, she's got her ball.
	She's got her ball, she's got her ball, etc.

2. *Imaginative play*

The scene is a bus stop on a cold day. There is a lady waiting for a bus. She is also waiting for a friend.

Lady	I'm glad the bus is late.
	My friend is late too.
	If she doesn't hurry she'll miss the bus.

She alternates between looking along the road for the bus and looking behind for her friend. Every now and then she looks at her watch and sometimes she shivers and swings her arms.

Monitor	What is she waiting for?
Chorus	The bus.
Monitor	Whom is she waiting for?
Chorus	Her friend.
Monitor	Is the bus late?
Chorus	Yes, it is.
Monitor	Are they both late?
Chorus	Yes, they are.
Monitor	Why is she swinging her arms?
Chorus	Because it's cold.
Monitor	What else does she do?
Chorus	Looks at her watch.
	Looks for her friend.
	Looks for the bus, etc.

These last responses and possibly some unexpected ones are likely to come all at the same time, unless once again a leader is used. (See the next section for another way of using the leader.) But perhaps here where there are so few possible responses, this does not matter very much. It is of course obvious that the more fluent the children become the less useful is chorus answering of this kind. This is why the whole technique is essentially one for the early stages of language learning.

Lady	Brr! It's cold. I wish my friend and the bus would come.
	Oh dear! Here comes the bus. My friend is not here, so she'll miss it.
Monitor	Whatever will she do?
	Will she get on the bus without her friend or will she wait for her friend and miss the bus too?
Chorus Leader	I think she'll get on the bus.
Chorus Leader (asking another member of the chorus)	
	What do you think?
Member	I think so too.
Member (to another)	
	What do you think?
Member	I think she will wait for her friend, etc.
Monitor	Let's watch her.

The lady puts her arm out to stop the bus and then looks suitably dismayed when it goes past.

Lady	Well! After all this waiting the bus is full. It's gone right past.

Suddenly she spots her friend at the back of the bus.

Lady	Hey! Stop! Oh dear! There is my friend on the bus. She has gone without me. And this is the last bus. I'll just have to walk. Oh well! Maybe the walk will warm me up.

She walks off in the direction which the bus took.

Monitor	Did she catch the bus?
Chorus	No, she didn't.
Monitor	Did her friend catch the bus?
Chorus	Yes, she did.

At this stage some more speculation is required about what happened, and also perhaps about what might happen when the friends finally meet. The 'What do you think?' structure is useful once again and monitor and chorus leader should start this off, gradually bringing in the other members of the chorus, which ceases to *be* one at this point. The ideas expressed such as:

> Her friend forgot to meet her.
> She didn't want to meet her.
> She got on at the stop before.
> They met later/the next day.
> They quarrelled, etc.

could well give rise to further community happenings, and indeed the whole experience might be a useful basis for some limited work in reading and writing.

87

Conclusion

It is hoped that these suggestions will help teaching teams to make use of the community happening as a large-group focusing technique. As with all focusing, it must take into account the field the children are actually experiencing and this, as has been stressed before, means careful thought and planning on the part of the teachers. If the field has been analysed and a language checklist agreed upon, the content of happenings is all there. What remains is the planning and rehearsal of procedure, with special attention to the balance between practice to consolidate old work and focusing to establish what is new and challenging. The community happening, as defined here, is a technique worthy of further exploration.

Further Reading

Garvie E. M. 'Language Happenings' in *Child Education* August 1973

Also

Byrne, D. *Progressive Picture Compositions* Longman 1967

6
Story-telling and Other Useful Techniques

Introduction

It is surprising how early in the development of a second language a child can begin to enjoy stories, provided that great care is taken to make the material interesting by selective use of themes, language and visuals. The story, with its marked sequence of events, its capacity for encouraging participation and its usefulness as a potential topic for related activities in other areas of the curriculum, is perhaps one of the most useful vehicles for language work. Vocabulary, sentence structure, changes of tense and other rules, pronunciation and rhythm, and the special language appropriate to particular purposes, can all be covered. With careful focusing techniques the teacher can extend the child's use of language and increase his fluency.

But the work must be well planned, again preferably by a team, making good use of their language checklist. There are problems of which many teachers in the normal school situation are not fully aware, problems not only of language but also of choice of topic and visual aids. The following quotation from the Bradford report, *English as a Second Language for the 5-year-old* illustrates the point. This concerned a teachers' workgroup which had been producing story materials.

The group found that their difficulties were threefold, those connected with the theme, the language and the illustration. The original story was written in a complicated way, and the pictures, though beautifully coloured and executed, were too full of detail to be meaningful to young children with limited language experience.

The first decision to be made was whether or not to use the theme at all. Were the concepts too difficult? It was decided that they need not be. If appropriately and sufficiently illustrated it was felt that the children could benefit from the story. . . . (Here followed some examples from the actual story under discussion.)

In considering the language and illustrations the group themselves learned a great deal. They began to realise, for instance, how confusing a teacher's language can be to a child, and the language in many books written for children. Often the illustrations are also confusing, where artistry has come before clarity.

On the matter of language even books which claim to control the vocabulary, sometimes pay little attention to the syntax, and the variety and complexity of the latter where several ideas are 'embedded' in one sentence, soon lose the interest of the listener at an early level of learning.

Consider the following, for example. 'But what interested Little Red Riding Hood most of all was the wolf she met in the wood', or again, 'If the wolf had not been so sorry to leave her, he would have been delighted to go home'. These sentences illustrate the 'flash forward' and the 'flash back' in thought and the necessity of using complicated tense forms.

Sometimes the teachers began with a theme and worked language appropriate to it out; sometimes they began with language they wanted to teach and selected a suitable theme as vehicle. Both approaches are useful. Let us consider now the adaptation of a traditional story which provided the Bradford teachers with a suitable theme. It was selected because of its clear sequencing of the stages of the story and because each part of the sequence allowed for useful repetition of ideas and language.

An adapted story

The story is usually called, 'The Old Woman Who Lived In A Vinegar Bottle'. Here the word 'vinegar' is left out and the story told as follows:

Once upon a time there was an old woman who lived in a bottle.
One day she was very sad. She was crying.
Suddenly a fairy came. 'What's the matter?' he asked.
'I don't want to live in a bottle,' the old woman said, 'I want
to live in a little house.'
So the fairy said, 'Stand up, shut your eyes, turn round three
times and open your eyes.'
So she stood up, she shut her eyes, she turned round three times
and she opened her eyes. And she was in a little house.
She was very happy. She was smiling.
Then, one day, she was crying again.
Suddenly the fairy came again. 'What's the matter now?' he asked.
'I don't want to live in a little house,' the old woman said, 'I
want to live in a big house.'
So the fairy said, 'Stand up, shut your eyes, etc.'
So she stood up, etc. And she was in a big house.
She was very happy. She was smiling.
Then one day she was crying again.
Suddenly the fairy came again, etc.
'I don't want to live in a big house,' the old woman said, 'I want
to live in a castle.'
So the fairy said, etc.
So she stood up, etc. And she was in a castle.
She was very happy. She was smiling.
Then one day, etc.
Suddenly the fairy came again, etc.
'I don't want to live in a castle,' the old woman said, 'I want to
live in a palace.'
So the fairy said, etc.
So she stood up, etc.
But she was not in a palace, she was not in a castle, she was not
in a big house, she was not in a little house. She was back in the
bottle and the fairy never came again.

The teaching aids for this story consist of an illustrated booklet and a
set of figurines with background sheets for a magnet-board. The teacher
when telling the story, and the emphasis is on telling not reading, either
turns the pages of the book slowly as the story unfolds, or builds up the
pictures with the figurines on the magnet-board. Timing is very
important so that the appropriate picture is shown linked to the
language it illustrates. The teacher can prolong each part of the
sequence by inserting extra language as follows:

Once upon a time there was an old woman
who lived in a bottle.
Look, here she is. Here is the bottle. The old
woman lives in the bottle. She is sitting
in a chair. Here is her table and here is
her cat, etc.

Learning/Teaching points

In other words the story as written is a guideline, or spine if you like,
which can be filled out with further material to suit the needs and level of
the children listening. Also the language already used can be varied to
suit these needs. For example, the fairy might say, 'What's the matter
this time?' instead of 'What's the matter now?', or the phrase, 'all at
once' might be substituted for 'suddenly' and the phrase, 'once more'
for 'again'. Obviously all these changes should not be introduced at the
same time but gradually, one at a time, as the story becomes familiar.

It is interesting how very quickly the young child begins to participate
in the telling of this story. Depending on how much care the teacher
gives to her own part in such things as tone of voice, facial expression,
gesture and actions in general, she will find the children crying and
smiling along with the old woman and getting increasingly exasperated
along with the fairy. And this is all a very important aspect of language.
These things can only be shown in context.

Also the teacher can very soon leave it to the children to say, 'Stand
up, shut your eyes, turn round three times and open your eyes' with the
appropriate changes to the past tense in the next part. They love this
constant repetition. Another useful thing is the way in which they
quickly begin to anticipate what comes next. The teacher might pause on
'And' for example, and the children will supply, 'she was in a big house'
or possibly only 'big house' so that the teacher must then say, 'Yes, she
was in a big house'. The three words, 'so', 'and' and 'but' are all
important here. Again they can only be taught in context and this
particular story is excellent for showing their use and what they imply in
English.

Notice the use of 'not' and 'never' in the last sequence. This is also
important. Very often the negative forms are not given enough
emphasis in language teaching. It is particularly necessary to give

92

practice with the 'not' form in English as many languages have only one way of expressing what English covers by 'no' and 'not'.

Finally the expressions, 'once upon a time', 'one day' and 'suddenly' have been deliberately introduced here, not because they are particularly important in every-day English or because they are very productive for the young child, but because they are appropriate for story-telling and it will be remembered that we must be concerned with the appropriateness of language even if it is very situational-bound. The same expressions should come into other stories so that they become formulae for story-telling.

Field, focus and extension

Although story-telling can be a way of focusing on language within the wide field of the curriculum, the use of a story can in itself, illustrate the notion of field and focus. The initial telling is the introductory limited field and the further concentrated language work is the real focus. This then can be followed by some elaboration and exploitation of the original story which widens the field leading to further focus and so on.

Already we have seen how the language of the spine can be filled out and varied. To be really helpful the illustrations should be altered accordingly. This is where the magnet-board figurines are particularly useful. It is not so easy to make changes in a book. With the story told here some extra figurines were devised to bring in new elements and points for discussion. For instance the fairy was depicted in different positions. He was made to sit in the old woman's chair and he was made to sit on the floor with his legs crossed. The old woman was shown holding the fairy's wand. She was also shown in another figure wearing an unaccustomed apron. There were two tables, one with a blue cloth and a jug on it and the other with a white cloth and a teapot on it. There were also two cats, one holding a mouse in its paw and the other licking its paw, having eaten the mouse perhaps.

Before exploiting the story to bring in these new elements the teacher must make sure that the original material is fully understood and all the possible language points have been covered. At the end of the book of pictures there is an extra sheet containing small pictures of the things and people that come into the original story. The teacher focuses on these, helping the children to identify, qualify and relate, and this might be done on several occasions with possible retelling of the story between focusing sessions, before any extension were attempted. And then, surreptitiously one or more new elements would be introduced and the whole process would begin again.

One last point worth noting about the extensions is that they have been deliberately designed to make the children look for samenesses and differences, an important thing for all young children building their basic concepts but particularly so where a second language is involved. It is also a vital concomitant of the pre-reading stage and its use here illustrates the point made earlier about the link with other areas of the curriculum.

A devised story

It is not always necessary to have different material for different levels of learning. Sometimes the same story and visuals can be used in different ways by the skilful teacher, depending on the ability of the children. Here now is an example of a story devised by a teacher. It is based on a series of four pictures which the teacher can draw herself or have drawn by someone else. The first shows a cat about to leap on to a table on which there is a jug of milk, the second shows the cat with its head in the tilted jug and some milk spilt on the table-cloth, the third shows a lady in the doorway and the cat poised for flight and the last shows the cat disappearing through the window with the lady by the table looking crossly at the spilt milk.

First of all let us imagine a situation where the group of children is at what we have called the Cracking the code stage. The teacher wants to revise in particular the present continuous form of the verb and the present simple. She also wants to practise the 'going to' form of the future. With the children looking at the pictures she might tell the story as follows:

THE NAUGHTY CAT

The cat is going to jump on to the table.
It wants a drink of milk.
Oh dear! The cat's head is in the milk-jug.
It is drinking the milk.
There is some milk on the table-cloth
Here comes a lady. The cat is frightened.
It is going to run away.
Now it is jumping out of the window.
The lady is looking at the milk-jug.
She is very cross.

Having told the story the teacher could then go on to focus upon the language by using a question and answer dialogue such as the following, either supplying the correct answers herself in the first instance or eliciting the help of a colleague as has been advocated earlier.

DIALOGUE

Q. What is the cat going to do here?
A. It's going to jump on to the table.
Q. What does it want?
A. It wants a drink of milk.
Q. What is the cat doing now?
A. It's drinking the milk.
Q. What is it going to do now?
A. It's going to run away.
Q. Why is it going to run away?
A. Because it's frightened.
Q. Why is it frightened.
A. Because there is a lady at the door.
Q. What is the cat doing now?
A. It's jumping out of the window.
Q. What is the lady doing here?
A. She is looking at the jug.
Q. Is she pleased?
A. No, she's not. She's very cross.

Notice that this particular story resulted from the teacher starting with the language she wanted to cover and then finding a suitable theme. Most of the language is highly productive. That is to say it demonstrates patterns used very frequently in everyday English. Even the expression, 'Here comes ———', which is appropriate here, shows a pattern of inversion which is used fairly frequently.

At other levels

If it were so desired, of course, the story could be treated in the same way as the one about the bottle, with new elements included to extend the original field and further focusing done on these. Perhaps the reader would like to try devising some of these extensions for more advanced levels of learners, possibly bringing in the simple past and the present perfect tenses. But for now, let us look at two other ways of dealing with the original four pictures. In both these examples let us suppose that the children are in the third of our three stages, the Breakthrough to fluency stage. They are able to use English fairly flexibly and the teacher can speak to them in almost the same manner as she would to native English speakers.

Example 1

The children are shown all four pictures. They are told that they tell a story and they are given a little time to study them. The focusing session which follows is very different from the previous one with children at an earlier stage. (N.B. It is not being suggested that the same children are involved here, even at a later stage of their learning. For this technique the children must come to the pictures for the first time.) Here the teacher aims to give the children as much freedom of expression as possible because they are able to cope with this. But it requires very skilful handling by the teacher. She cannot predict what the children are going to say and she must be ready to give the most appropriate prompt at the right moment. Here is a possible sequence:

Teacher	What is the story about?
Child	About a cat.
Teacher	Yes, tell me more.
Child	It wants to drink the milk.
Teacher	So what happens?
Child	It jumps on to the table and it puts its head in the jug and the jug falls over.
Teacher	Good. What else?
Child	Some milk is spilt.
Teacher	Then?
Child	A lady comes and the cat is scared.
Teacher	So?
Child	It runs away.

96

Teacher	Where to?
Child	Out of the window. It goes into the garden.
Teacher	What does the lady do?
Child	She looks at the spilt milk. She says, 'Oh, you naughty cat.'

It can be readily seen that the whole style of this dialogue is different from that of the last. It is a natural conversation which might be heard in any British classroom. The main difference is in the use of abbreviated structures, especially on the part of the teacher, but even the child uses these, for example, 'About a cat' and 'Out of the window'. This is perfectly good English but competence to abbreviate appropriately can only come from competence to use the full structures, and children must go through the early stage first.

Another interesting point is the constant use of the simple present tense form, for example, 'it wants', and 'the lady comes'. Again this is a stage of learning reached. It is a matter of style. What has been learnt, in addition to the actual form itself, is that this is often used in English for the telling of a story or for description of events, even sometimes when the events have happened in the past. It makes the telling more vivid and exciting. Consider the football commentary. The commentator might say, 'Jones passes the ball to Smith and Smith passes it to Black', etc., even if grammatically it would be more correct to use 'is passing' or 'passed' depending on the time of the telling. Again this matter of choice of style can only be handled when the basic work of learning the range of tense forms has been done.

Example 2

In the next sequence the children are shown the pictures one by one and the aim is to have them anticipate events, to make guesses and to use words like 'might', 'maybe' and 'perhaps'. This is quite a sophisticated use of language and it matches the stage of thought which the children should by now have reached, what we have called the Manipulation stage, where they are able to look back and forward in time and to consider the possible. We saw something of this in the last chapter in the role-play about the lady waiting for the bus. The dialogue here might be something like the following:

First picture

Teacher	What do you think the cat is going to do?
Child	Jump on the table.
Teacher	Why?
Child	Maybe he wants to eat something, or he might want to drink some milk.

Second picture

Teacher	What *is* he doing?
Child	Drinking milk.
Teacher	Guess what happens next.
Child 1	He gets his head stuck in the jug.
Child 2	The jug breaks and there is a lot of blood because the cat gets cut.
Child 3	Perhaps somebody comes in and chases the cat.
Child 4	Maybe the person falls over the cat and breaks his leg.
Teacher	What might happen then?
Child 4	The cat would run away and the person would go to hospital.

Third picture

Teacher	Who *does* come in?
Child	A lady.
Teacher	What do you think the cat is going to do now?
Child	Run away.

Fourth picture

Teacher	What might the cat do now?
Child 1	Hide in the bushes.
Child 2	Never come back.
Teacher	What do you think the lady is saying to herself?
Child 1	What a naughty cat!
Child 2	I must not leave the milk on the table again.

As in the last sequence the style is one of natural English between teacher and child, but notice that this time the teacher uses most of the full structures and the child uses the majority of the abbreviated ones, except when making guesses which really challenge the imagination. This is an interesting change. In the previous dialogue the aim was to encourage free expression so the teacher 'holds back' as it were. In this one which is possibly a step further on, the teacher knows the children *can* express themselves freely. The aim here is to encourage a new kind of thinking and the use of particular language. She must therefore give more language help herself.

The fact that the child uses fuller structures when making his more imaginative guesses is also interesting. This bears out what has been said before about the important place of language in relation to thought. When the message is obvious he can afford to be economical with words and the teacher can afford to accept the shortened form. When some hard thinking has to be done more language help is needed for the ordering of thought.

Related activities

A story, whether adapted or devised, whether theme or language orientated, can become the centre-piece of a whole host of interesting activities. Many lend themselves to role-play and drama which can be enhanced by the imaginative use of sound effects on tape or record. Take, for example, the story of *Jack and the Beanstalk*. Once this has been adapted to the needs of the second language learner and treated in the manner suggested above so that the children are fully familiar with the story and able to use the language involved, an enthusiastic team of teachers could further adapt it for drama and movement.

Drama and movement

The beauty of this kind of activity is that all the children can be involved, either as narrators, or actors, or 'Greek chorus' (see below) or even as parts of the scenery. For instance, in the part where Jack climbs up the beanstalk and makes his way to the giant's castle, a boy, acting as Jack, is put perhaps on a box on a raised platform where he mimes climbing movements, and a girl stands below, looking up at him. Meanwhile suitable music is played on tape or record or perhaps on the piano, as background, while a small group of children led at first by a teacher, narrate as follows:

> Jack begins to climb the beanstalk.
> He climbs higher and higher.
> His mummy looks up.
> She sees him climbing higher and higher.
> Jack looks down.
> He sees his mummy getting smaller and smaller, etc.

99

The rest of the children are getting ready for the moment when Jack reaches the top of the beanstalk and enters his enchanted forest. Apart from the boy who will play the part of the giant and the girl who will be his wife, the children become the trees of the forest, waving their branches in the wind and making Jack's passage through them difficult and frightening. Again suitable music should be found to accompany this drama and the trees themselves, joined by the original narrators, can chant their comments on the events in the way the chorus did in the plays of ancient Greece. For example:

> The wind is blowing.
> The wind is shaking the trees,
> Faster and faster.
> Jack is running.
> Now he is creeping.
> The wind is moaning,
> Whoo-oo-oo.
> Jack is frightened.
> He can't see. It's dark, etc.

The important thing, from the point of view of language work, is that all this movement and music should really support both theme and language which are already familiar. It may be that once the drama is planned some new vocabulary or even special formulae suggest themselves as relevant. The word 'moaning' in the above is an example here. This is all to the good provided the new material is carefully controlled. The aim must always be to enhance what has already been learnt, and skilfully handled, there is nothing more effective than the use of drama and music where the child can react to tune and rhythm with his whole body.

Still on the subject of drama, this time perhaps without music, many stories lend themselves to the kind of community happenings described in Chapter 5 where teachers act out the tale and the monitor leads the community in response, helped by the chorus leader and the other adults dispersed amongst the children. The story about the bottle could well be treated in this way.

Puppets

Another idea is to use puppets and these do not need to be complicated

100

tangles of string. They can be simple home made sock or glove puppets. The children themselves can quickly learn to manipulate them and to be the voices behind the scenes. For shy children still unsure of themselves in the second language, puppets are an extremely helpful device because it is the puppet who 'sounds funny' and makes the mistakes. Puppet plays are often better to be those devised by teachers and they lend themselves to short situations based on specific language to be covered. For example:

Greetings

Puppet 1	Hello. What's your name?
Puppet 2	Hello. My name's Ayub.
	What's your name?
Puppet 1	My name's Balbir.

Yes it is/No, it isn't

Puppet 1	This is Monday.
Puppet 2	No, it isn't.
Puppet 1	Yes, it is.
Puppet 2	No, it isn't. It's Tuesday.

Yes, he is/No, he isn't

One of the puppets could act as monitor for chorus work here as in the community happenings. Puppet 1 could give instructions to Puppet 2 and sometimes mistakes could be made, as follows:

Puppet 1	Put your hands up.
Puppet (to chorus)	Is he right?
Chorus	Yes, he is.
Puppet 1	Put your hands on your head.
Puppet (to chorus)	Is he right?
Chorus	No, he isn't, etc.

Rhymes and songs

It will be remembered that in the story about the bottle one of the most useful parts for language teaching was the fairy's instruction to the old woman which was repeated over and over again. This kind of thing appears in many stories, for example:

Run, run, as fast as you can.
You can't catch me.
I'm the gingerbread man.

or

He huffed and he puffed,
And he blew the house down.

This constant repetition of enjoyable language with careful attention to all the stresses and intonation patterns is very valuable. It is the particular strength of rhymes and songs whether or not they are connected with stories. Consider the following song which is based on a story but which, for the Bradford teachers, developed along its own particular lines and even became the topic for other activities in the curriculum.

ZOZO THE MONKEY

1. Zozo the monkey is clapping his hands.
   He's clapping his hands.
   He's clapping his hands.
   Zozo the monkey is clapping his hands.
   He's clapping his hands today.
2. Zozo the monkey is washing his face, etc.
3. Zozo the monkey is nodding his head, etc.

A glove puppet of a monkey is useful here and the children are encouraged to imitate his actions while they sing. As with a story the theme and language of a song can be exploited and used for all sorts of purposes but let us look first at the language which can be focused upon already, for example:

(a) the present continuous tense is clapping/washing/nodding
(b) names for parts of the body hands/face/head
(c) the singular (male) pronoun
    and possessive he, his

The teacher might ask a boy to perform the same actions as Zozo and then the children would be asked questions such as:

What is he doing?
What's this? (touching head/face)

Zozo the Mon-key is clapping his hands. (Key of D)

Zo-zo the mon-key is clapp-ing his hands, He's clapp-ing his hands, He's clapp-ing his hands.

Zo-zo the mon-key is clapp-ing his hands, He's clapp-ing his hands to - - - day.

What are these? (touching hands)
What's that (pointing to head/face)
What are those? (pointing to hands)

Extension of this initial field could be provided by giving Zozo a sister so that the female pronoun 'she' could be covered and the possessive 'her'. The plural 'they' and 'them' could also be used. In addition, Zozo's original actions could be added to, to increase the use of verb vocabulary.

And the theme could be carried into other activities. In pre-reading work, for instance, the children might be shown a series of pictures of Zozo where one shows him doing something different. The aim here is visual discrimination, and the fact that the children are already familiar with Zozo and his activities, makes it possible for them to concentrate on the task in hand which is to find the odd man out.

Again, in the same area of the curriculum, a jigsaw of Zozo performing one of his activities could be devised.

As a more extended activity bringing in new vocabulary, a counting rhyme could be used, linking number work and drama, as follows:

> Five little monkeys came out to play,
> Eating bananas along the way.
> Out came a tiger, orange and black,
> Four little monkeys went running back.

This rhyme could be developed into a story illustrated by a series of pictures and handled in the same way as *The Naughty Cat*.

Another song which proved popular with the Bradford teachers is:

Three Brown Sparrows.　(Original key B) Key of C

Three brown spa-rrows,　　three brown spa-rrows,

three brown spa - rrows　sitt-ing on a wall

Say: "One flew away. Aw!" Then sing: "Two brown sparrows" etc.

THREE BROWN SPARROWS

> Three brown sparrows,
> Three brown sparrows,
> Three brown sparrows sitting on a wall.

The use of the magnet-board is suggested. There should be a section of wall and three figurines of sparrows coloured brown. The first verse is sung and then someone takes one sparrow away. When the action is complete all say:

> One flew away. Aw!

The singing is then continued:

> Two brown sparrows,
> Two brown sparrows,
> Two brown sparrows sitting on a wall.

Somebody removes another sparrow and all say:

> Another one flew away. Aw!

> One brown sparrow, etc.

The last sparrow is removed and all say:

> The third sparrow flew away. Aw!

> No brown sparrows,
> No brown sparrows,
> No brown sparrows sitting on a wall.

The sparrows are brought back one by one and the following is sung and said by all:

> One came back. Hurray!
> One brown sparrow,
> One brown sparrow,
> One brown sparrow sitting on a wall.
> Another one came back. Hurray!
> Two brown sparrows, etc.
> The third one came back. Hurray!
> Three brown sparrows, etc.

Notice here once again the careful sequencing of events and language, for example 'one', 'another one' and 'the third one'. Notice too the constant repetition of words and structures. For many children also the consonant clusters at the beginning of 'three' and 'sparrow' are a problem. This song provides useful practice.

An interesting idea is to sing the first three verses progressively more slowly and sadly and the last three progressively more quickly and happily. The aim is to contrast the negative and positive aspects which are also emphasised by the use of the exclamations 'Aw!' and 'Hurray!'

Music generally

Perhaps the most important thing which rhymes and songs have to offer the language learner is the beat which runs through the lines. This is present all the time in language, closely linked with the rise and fall of the voice, all of which can be very important to meaning and the learner has to acquire these things along with everything else he is learning about the language. Verse and music generally are invaluable aids in this concern.

Putting particular structures to music and beating out the rhythm is a useful exercise. For example, to the tune of *Three Blind Mice*:

> One, two, three,
> What can you see?

Three Blind Mice   (Original key B♭) Key of C

Three blind mice. Three blind mice. See how they

run, See how they run, they all run af-ter the

farmer's wife, who cut off their tails with a carv-ing knife; did

ev-er you see such a thing in your life, as three

blind mice!

Someone could beat the rhythm on a drum and the children could be asked to clap their hands while they sing. Notice that these two lines bring out an important thing about English stress. Their total length is the same but the second line has more words. The two words 'can you' have to be rushed together to fit in. This is often difficult for the foreign speaker whose language may be stressed differently. In stretching out the pattern by singing it, we can perhaps make it easier to learn.

A little game could be played here with the guessing-bag. An interesting object should be produced each time the song is sung and the children or one child should reply, 'I can see a ——'. The children too can hold the bag in turn and produce the objects. Vocabulary is also being practised and the objects used should be carefully chosen for the purpose, new things being introduced gradually as the names are learned.

All kinds of percussion instruments can be used for work on the rhythm of language, and other things such as piano or recorder can be helpful for discrimination work on pitch. The children could be asked to listen to different sequences of notes and to perceive samenesses and differences. One member of staff could perhaps make this her special area and might record on tape the exercises found to be most useful for the pupils concerned.

Further use of dialogues

So important are these aspects of spoken English that they are worth considering a little further. Is there any other technique that could be used besides the use of rhymes, songs and musical instruments? Here is an idea that might be tried either as a community happening or as role-play in a small group. It is a further elaboration of the dialogue work described in Chapter 4.

The theme sentence is 'What do you want?' Try ringing the changes as follows:

1

Situation:

One person is sitting at a table on which are placed a number of articles familiar to the children. Another comes in and stands looking at the articles. This first dialogue is the same as the first one in Chapter 4.

Speaker 1	What do you want?
Speaker 2	May I have a ball/pencil, etc., please?
Speaker 1	Yes, here you are.
Speaker 2	Thank you.

107

There must be lots of practice first by adults and then by children of this simple little dialogue before going on to the following:

2
Situation:

The same procedure except that the person making the request speaks so quietly that the one at the table cannot hear the first time.

> Speaker 1 (in a whisper)   May I have a ball/pencil, etc., please?
>
> Speaker 2 (with some
>
>   irritation)   *What* do you want?

The reader should try saying this with the stress laid on the first word. It will be noticed that the slight pause which follows means that the word 'do' tends to sound more as it would if said in isolation than it does in the previous dialogue. There it sounds more like 'di'. This is an important point to notice about pronunciation. It alters in continuous speech according to the stress and pausing.

3
Situation:

This time the person making the request is not sure what she wants. She keeps changing her mind.

> Speaker 1   May I have a ball—no—a pencil—no—, etc.
>
> Speaker 2   (again with some irritation)
>
>   What *do* you want?

Notice the complete change in the intonation here when the stress is moved to the second word, and the fact that the stressed word 'do' really does have its full value. Stress and intonation are very closely linked. Where one alters so does the other.

4
Situation:

Several people have come in to ask for things as in the first situation above. Finally the person at the table begins to get tired. The next person who comes in is greeted by the question:

> What do *you* want?

Here the implication is, 'Oh dear! Here's another person to bother me.' Note that there could be another implication here. It could also mean, 'I don't like you'.

5

Situation:

The person coming into the room roams about apparently aimlessly for a while and does not ask for anything. She might appear to be searching for something. The person at the table watches for a while and then says:

What do you *want*?

The implication in this case is that I know you want something but I don't know what it is.

The native speaker of English makes all these changes quite unconsciously. The ability to do so has been acquired during the early years of socialisation in the English-speaking community. Non-English speakers also acquire their own particular devices for indicating underlying implications, and the young children with whom we are concerned here may have mastered quite a number of these already. They now have to learn the English patterns, but obviously *not* by explanation and discussion. With adult learners this is possible and perhaps helpful. With little children, experience of them in meaningful context is the most we can provide. It is certainly worth trying and there is one great asset which young children possess and that is the ability to imitate without any inhibitions or self-consciousness. The teacher should make full use of this.

Conclusion

In this chapter we have ranged over a number of techniques. Through stories, drama and music, etc., the aim is to link experience and language. The ideas suggested here are merely pointers to what might be attempted by an enthusiastic and imaginative team. Many more could have been given. For instance, little has been said about the use of games. These too, 'active' and 'table'; noisy and quiet, offer endless opportunities for language work. But this area would require a chapter to itself. Suggestions for further reading have been given.

The important point to remember about all this work is that whatever is done, it should be understood by the children at *their* level of language development and they should be able to take an active part both linguistically and socially. Theme, language and illustration are the three elements of the learning/teaching situation mentioned by the Bradford teachers' story group and the skilled teacher must be able to manipulate them in such a way that optimum learning is achieved. In the next chapter we will look more closely at the third element, illustration.

Further Reading

Leclerc, M. *Strategies, Activities and Games for Language Work* City of Bradford Metropolitan Council Directorate of Educational Services 1975
Lee, W. R. *Language Teaching Games and Contests* Oxford University Press 1965

Also

English as a Second Language for the 5-Year-Old City of Bradford Educational Services Committee Autumn 1973

7
Illustrative Materials

Introduction

So much of what the child learns comes to him through his eyes. This is why, in teaching, visual aids are an important part of the equipment, and language teaching is no exception. The picture, in a variety of forms, can be invaluable to the child in the interpretation of spoken messages. Sometimes it helps to confirm and consolidate learning; sometimes it helps to shed light on something new. In the same way that a rhyme or song is, as it were, a little 'package' of language for the child to play with and enjoy, so the picture is a 'package' of experience caught and held for him to linger over. If the 'packages' of language and experience are carefully matched and put together they offer truly valuable learning material.

The problem of matching language and picture highlights, in fact, the wider problem which this book is all about, that of linking language and experience in general. We become more and more conscious of a basic paradox which is hard to resolve. On the one hand the child needs experience to help him to understand language, and on the other he needs language to help him to understand experience. In other words, experience gives content and meaning to the noises the child hears when people speak, but if new experience is to be adequately interpreted and absorbed, the child needs the tool of language for labelling, qualifying, relating, classifying and generally manipulating his thinking. The teacher requires to be able to assess the degree and complexity of the experience the child can cope with linguistically. This is problem enough but for the teacher of the second-language learner there is an added difficulty. It is hard for her to know if a child's apparent difficulty is due to lack of language fluency in general or lack of fluency in the second language in particular. He may be able to use language as a thinking tool very efficiently in his mother-tongue but not as yet in the new code. Perhaps as we focus now on the use of pictures in language teaching we may begin to understand the wider problem more clearly and to realise the importance of planning very carefully the kind of experience we present to children.

Pictures should be used from the early stages of learning a second language. Almost as soon as the child begins to recognise and label the real objects in his environment it is expedient to show him representations of them for further practice and consolidation. For instance, the first objects used in the language 'kit-bag' should all have their pictorial counterparts. This is of course also an important pre-reading step. In company with the native speaker, the second-language learner has eventually to be able to recognise the representation of sounds as graphic symbols, and both have to be guided towards this final step. For the second-language learner, as has been emphasised before, much more time must be spent in the beginning on oral practice, and pictures provide the child with a quick and easy means of constant revision. They also help to support the learning of new material and they help to widen the environment by bringing the outside world into the classroom.

Obviously there are a great many different kinds of visuals which can be used for a variety of purposes. Teaching teams should build up their own particular 'libraries' of illustrative material which they have adopted, adapted and devised, including also pictures which children have produced. The great value of team-work here is that differing artistic gifts can be made to complement each other. Sometimes too, interested friends and relations, both of staff and children, can be encouraged to assist. The collection will be a constant source from which to draw, but it should be continually brought up-to-date, as new circumstances require special treatment, and it should be carefully stored for easy access, the visuals being made as durable as possible with the use of such things as transpaseal and plastic bags. Transparent covering is also useful for quick recognition of contents. In addition, teachers should file, for future reference, notes on the purposes which the pictures have successfully fulfilled and on the techniques which helped to further those purposes.

Differences of kind and purpose

The kind of illustrative material used will, of course, depend on the aim in view. One important attribute is size. Bearing in mind that work is done with large groups, with small groups and with individuals, teachers should have pictures suitable for all three situations. Small pictures can be used with large groups if they are projected, as we shall see later. For small-group work, pictures about the size of A4 paper are very suitable and for work with individuals, it is useful to have some the size of playing cards. These can be easily manipulated by the children themselves, and some can be used for games such as Picture Bingo and Snap. There are of course also the small pictures which appear in books but some of these are not at all appropriate for the second-language learner and teachers should try to make their own books, including the concertina kind which can stand on a table or shelf.

Pictures can also be coloured or black and white, and it is wise to make careful selection here. Time and space do not allow for a discussion of the various psychological arguments for and against the use of colour, but teachers should be aware of them. Sometimes colour lends interest and furthers learning; sometimes it distracts and hinders it. There are times, of course, when colour itself is the main area of learning, in which case it must be used. Again, however, it should be carefully deployed to ensure that the child will focus on the relevant things.

This brings in the question of degree of clarity in general. Often those who illustrate for children commercially, in books or elsewhere, are motivated by the idea of enrichment and aesthetic effect and they allow their imaginations full rein. For some children pictures of this kind are exciting and challenging. They are capable of the kind of thinking which can sort out the wood from the trees and they can express their findings to the teacher in fluent language. For others, much of the artistic detail is a distraction. Either they do not possess the flexibility of thought with which to make sense of the picture or they have not the fluency in the language of school which will enable them to voice their thoughts, or both. Whichever is the case, it is unfair to present these children with a piece of experience which immediately puts them at a disadvantage. For them something much clearer and simpler with less artistic 'clutter' will serve their present needs better, and there should be a gradual increase of complexity as they become able to cope. Bold line drawing is often best in the early stages.

There should be pictures to support situational language work and those which help particularly the learning of language structure. In practice both kinds should give the child scope for practising his use of language, but the teachers in preparing the material, start off with a different emphasis in each case. It will be remembered that the same was true, for example, of devising stories. This two-directional approach is an important principle in general for all language work. On the one hand we have to be concerned with situations and topics which demand that certain language be used, and on the other we have to be concerned about the structuring of language itself.

Situational pictures, for instance at the Initial orientation stage, could depict scenes of school such as the cloakroom or the dining-room. These would support the role-play being done in the community happenings. At later stages visuals are required which illustrate stories, rhymes, songs, mathematical concepts such as ordering and all kinds of centres of interest taking the child beyond the school boundaries. And in addition to the actual situational pictures there should be accompanying sets which show individual objects and/or people concerned in the situations. For example, relating to the dining-room scene, there might be pictures of knife, fork, spoon, plate, etc. These two kinds of picture allow for work which fosters understanding of both the overall concept and its component parts, and which gives opportunities for practice of both appropriate patterns of language and vocabulary.

A further possibility is to have visual material which helps with understanding categories of experience cutting across the situations, things such as colour, size and shape, and others (see Chapter 3, p. 51) such as parts of the body, kinship and occupations. An extension of this idea which could also include pictures of the component parts of situations as suggested above, would be to have the same pictures utilised for special pre-reading work. They could, for example, be arranged in sets for matching and discrimination. As has been noted before, if a child is already familiar with the material he is handling he is in a better position to concentrate on the skill which it is supposed to be teaching. Here we can see once again the vital link between special

114

language work and all the other aspects of the child's development. The two must go forward together.

Pictures which help particularly the learning of language structure are often difficult both to find and devise and this task really must be the result of team-work. Teachers should try things out on one another and on other native speakers. It is important that the illustration shows exactly what the language means. For example it might be desirable to show the contrast of nearness and farness in the sentences, 'This is a book' and 'That is a book'. Two pictures side by side could illustrate a person (a) holding the book and (b) pointing to it. The same pictures, except that the person now has two books, could be used to show the singular/plural contrast and the use of 'these' and 'those'. Again it might be required to depict the difference between the present continuous tense form as in 'He is jumping' and the 'going to' future form as in 'He is going to jump'. Pairs of pictures in which the first shows a person or an animal actually doing the action and the second shows him/it about to do it, might be devised. But this is not always easy to do and much thought and care must go into the work. For ideas of what to illustrate, teachers should be guided by both their checklist and the particular difficulties of their own pupils, and the latter may even be incorporated into the checklist.

In a sense the next point has already been covered in passing but it is worth pin-pointing. Sometimes visuals come singly and sometimes in sets. The single wall-chart or frieze illustrating an overall centre of interest, for example, may be all that is needed to serve the purpose in hand, or the single smaller picture for work with a few or individual children. This may contain all the things the teacher wishes to focus on. In fact, it is sometimes useful to have one visual on which there are a limited number of talking points and to focus on each in turn. From the sheer practical point of view this saves both material and storage space, but also in terms of learning, it is often a good idea to place deliberately side by side, in physical proximity, representations of ideas which are related. These may be the component parts of a situation such as the knife, fork, etc., set, or sets in language structure such as 'this', 'that', 'these' and 'those'. For a way of helping the children to concentrate on each part in turn, see the description of the 'focuser' on p. 123.

Sets of pictures also have their special uses. In Chapter 6 we saw how they could be used in different ways for telling stories, for instance. The ordering of events can be made so much clearer by visual aids. Sometimes when a story has to be adapted and simplified, language and illustration can work together. There might be, for example, one picture in a book to illustrate the following sentence taken from a story:

Tommy, though he was carrying all his granny's groceries, began to walk, as the bus was not coming and it was raining, to the farm at the top of the hill.

With its use of subordinate clauses and connecting words such as 'though' and 'as', the sentence is extremely complex. There are several ideas all mixed up together and the mind has to jump backwards and forwards to make sense of them. The fluent language user can do this, but the learner still struggling with basic structure and vocabulary, has great difficulty.

It could be that if the picture is well executed, it will serve to make the sentence clear. On the other hand a picture in a book is likely to be fairly small and it is sometimes hard to see the relevant detail clearly. The teacher can do one of two things. She can either enlarge the picture given or she can make a series of pictures, each representing one of the ideas given in the sentence. If she chooses the latter she must first of all decide what these ideas are. They might be something like this for the above example:

Tommy was carrying all his granny's groceries.
The bus was not coming.
It was raining.
Tommy began to walk to the farm.
The farm was at the top of the hill.

The teacher must decide also whether or not to present the children with this breakdown of the language or to leave her set of pictures to do this work. It might well be that if the story is to be told to children of differing abilities, and the teacher should think hard about the advisability of doing this, then it would be useful to have both language and illustrations which would enable all the children to participate fully.

Sets of pictures can also be made to illustrate series of happenings in the school day or in the day of some well-known person. These are particularly useful for the development of the time sense and they can be used in conjunction with work on the simple present tense form,

116

especially the rather difficult third person singular, for example, 'goes' or 'gets up'. Time adverbial expressions such as 'every day' and 'each morning' can also be brought in here.

We have seen too how sets of pictures can be used for illustrating categories of experience. Teachers should be conscious all the time of the need for concept-building and these pictures give endless opportunities for identifying, qualifying, relating and classifying. In addition to classifying by content it is also useful to group pictures which have some language attribute in common. The objects might all begin with a vowel, for instance, so that in naming them the child has to learn to use 'an' instead of 'a'.

Finally sets of cut-out figures are useful, including reticulated figurines with movable parts. More will be said about these in connection with the use of the magnet-board. For quick manipulation and easy change from one event to another, the cut-outs have an undoubted advantage over the static picture. A set of figurines might represent the members of a family or a group of friends in a neighbourhood. All kinds of interesting things can be made to happen to these people by simply altering their arrangement. New illustrations are not necessary except perhaps for background sheets.

Another type of visual is the photograph. There is usually one member of a teaching team who is enthusiastic about photography. Some excellent support for topic work can be gained here especially if the children themselves can be brought into the pictures. Tremendous interest can be aroused. Outings and visits lend themselves to useful language work, provided the event is well prepared beforehand, the outing itself is not only interesting and enjoyable but carefully planned so that all the teachers know the field of learning it is supposed to be covering, and the follow-up, aided by photographs and perhaps other visuals, really focuses on this part of the field. The sets of photographs can also be used long after the visit itself is past to help the children to retain what was learnt from it. Slides and films are also possible. These will be mentioned again in the next section.

Nor must we forget the illustrative work done by the children themselves. Work in art and craft of all kinds can be used to aid in the development of language. From simple colouring, tracing, joining of dots, etc., to production of the more complicated and imaginative wall-

117

frieze or collage, there are opportunities for talk and concept-building. For instance the language of colour, shape and texture comes immediately to mind and the instrumental language related to the activities themselves. Work with plasticine and clay and materials of all kinds including junk, can produce interesting visual aids and provide many useful talking points. The children can provide their own illustrations for stories and events which have caught their attention. Even at a very early stage they can be asked to do simple follow-up tasks after language focusing sessions, such as colouring in a picture of a big ball and a little ball or tracing a number of objects they have just learnt to name. Teachers must be very patient in the beginning however. For children from some cultures, pencils, pens, brushes and scissors are very new gadgets and sometimes it takes a while for the necessary eye and hand co-ordination to develop. Before bringing this to the aid of language work it may be helpful to spend time on the skills alone, except of course for the language which is used in any learning activity.

Many of the things suggested above are already going concerns in a number of schools and the list is by no means exhaustive. But it is hoped that the reader will find something here which may stimulate a new train of thought. The main point to remember is that visual aids should be looked upon not as an extra, not only as attractive show-pieces to display on parents' day, but as an integral part of the children's learning experience.

'Hardware'

Teachers of young children often feel that the use of sophisticated teaching machines is not for them. Sometimes, especially nowadays, it is a question of finance. Very few first schools can afford to purchase costly equipment. On the other hand the real educational value of these things is often not realised. Teachers have perhaps not received much information about them in their initial training and have probably had even less experience of using them or of seeing them in use, especially with little children. This is something which could be rectified. The use of 'hardware' should also be included in in-service courses.

It is not intended here to go into the matter in any great detail, especially the technical aspects, but brief mention of one or two things

118

which can be useful to the first school teacher should perhaps be made, with particular reference to the context of this chapter.

Epidiascope and overhead projector

Sometimes a picture which just suits the moment is not large enough for all the children to see. This is where it is an advantage to be able to enlarge and project. The epidiascope is useful for this. Pictures in books or magazines, photographs or drawings, etc., can all be projected in the epidiascope and the teacher can use a pencil or a special pointer to indicate the part to be focused upon. For the overhead projector it is necessary to have specially prepared visuals but the time in planning and making can be well-spent. Many teachers' centres have a thermal copier where teachers can obtain 'one-off' copies or stencils. The latter are particularly useful as they can be used over and over again to make visuals for groups of children to use individually. It is even possible to make a black and white picture from a coloured original with the help of a photo-copier. The overhead projector can also be used, with special pens, for quick sketching and writing, in the same way as a chalkboard, but with the advantage that the teacher does not need to turn her back on her pupils.

All kinds of useful language work can be done, aided by projected visuals. For instance, in the early stages of learning, a set of pictures showing people doing different actions could be used, giving practice in the structures, 'Who's this?' and 'What is he/she doing?' The children could answer in chorus in much the same way as they do in the community happenings. This is a practice and consolidating activity and not one for introducing the language concerned. Of course the work could be done without the aid of a projector and many other ways should be found for practising structures, as this book has tried to show, but the special focusing required in this particular situation can stimulate interest and effort.

Story-telling can also benefit from this approach. One advantage is that if teachers are making the effort to prepare a set of 'frames' for the projector, they will be more likely to focus carefully on the matching of ideas to language and to make sure that what is presented really furthers understanding of the theme. Another is that in working with the children

119

a variety of techniques is possible. For instance the story can be allowed to go on without interruption, with the visuals complementing the voice, or there can be pauses while certain 'frames' are held so that the teacher can comment and question and/or the children can do the same before the story moves on and the talking-point is forgotten.

The use of accompanying sound effects, perhaps on a tape-recorder, is another possibility. But there has to be careful synchronisation. The sound might take the form simply of background music or of things specific to the activities going on in the pictures, such as the sounds of vehicles or water running. Apart altogether from story-telling it might be useful to have sets of visuals specially designed to match sounds. Pictures of animals could be shown accompanied by the noises they make. Finally it is often beneficial to have commentaries, even of the stories, on tape. This leaves the teacher freer to watch and to react to the responses of the children. It also gives the children experience of hearing voices other than those of their own teachers, if a number of adults can be persuaded to co-operate. People outside the school altogether might be asked to do some recordings. For instance the teen-age children of teachers might find this an interesting ploy. For many second-language learners the only standard English they ever hear is that spoken by their teachers and they must learn to react to different voices.

Slide, strip and film projector

Both home-made and commercial material in the form of slides, film-strips and cine-films, can be used. Slides and film-strips are usually better because they allow for pausing, a point mentioned above. Like photographs, material made on location is particularly useful, but teachers should examine the commercial catalogues for things which may be suitable for young children. Some of the Ladybird stories, for instance, have been filmed. Most teachers' centres keep catalogues and often they have a supply of film-strips, etc., for loan.

Day-light screen

This is another useful thing to have. It can be set up on a table in a corner of a room and used with a small projector. The advantages of

120

this for small group focusing can readily be seen. Even some of the children themselves might be able to work a small slide projector. It is surprising how adept and responsible small children can be in these matters and they should be encouraged to become so. If the teacher feels that she can safely leave a group of children or an individual to work with apparatus without help the learning/teaching situation is opened out considerably.

Language Master and Synchrofax

Take these two pieces of apparatus for example. An individual child can be set to work on tasks specially suited to his own needs. This is particularly useful in a multi-cultural class where there is likely to be a great variety of difficulties. But all teachers have to cope with individual differences and this equipment can be an asset in any classroom. Again there is matching of visual and verbal language. The Language Master uses strips of card and the teacher makes use of these as she wishes. At the turn of a knob the card moves through the machine showing the child either a picture or written words and a voice says something about what is being shown or reads the actual words.

The Synchrofax machine acts as a talking page. A magnetic sheet, again touched off very simply, presents both visual and sound. It might be a scene from a familiar story with the voice using a few key sentence patterns, or it could be a picture of one or two objects selected for their usefulness in supplying a special language focus. They might be set in different positions and the voice could say things like, 'The X is on the table' and 'The Y is under the chair'. It could also be the illustration for a rhyme or song where the language used might be for practice with some particular difficulty of pronunciation. A child with this difficulty could sit and play the 'page' over and over again possibly muttering the language to himself in company with the voice. There are endless possibilities.

Tape-recorder

Mention has been made several times already of this, perhaps the most useful gadget for language work. Here too the child can be left to

121

work on his own or a group can work together if an audio distributor unit or junction box is used. The latter consists of a means whereby several children, using ear-phones, can listen in to the same recording. Whole stories can be told while the child turns over the pages of a book of pictures. The use of tapes enables the teacher to devise stories at different levels of difficulty and perhaps to group children who are roughly at the same stage. A series of rhymes and songs could also be put on tape and again the children could have illustrations to look at as they listened.

Another use of the tape-recorder is as an instructor of simple tasks, though this requires closer supervision. The tape might contain directions for picture-matching or manipulation of objects such as animals in a farm-yard or dolls and furniture in a dolls' house. The child might complete a number of tasks and then call the teacher to check his work. For speed the teacher should have a specially prepared guide to refer to.

Many teachers of young children who at first were highly doubtful both about the educational value of 'hardware' where young children are concerned and about their own ability to use it adequately, have been converted and find their work greatly extended and enriched because of it. Some schools have even set up 'Listening Corners' or small bays where some of the gadgets for small-group and individual work, can be permanently kept and regularly used. It is recommended that those who are still amongst the doubters should (a) aim to see on-going work in places such as the Bradford Infant Centres where 'hardware' is much used successfully, (b) urge their local authorities to put on courses for training in the technical aspects, including devising materials or 'software' and (c) consult the appropriate catalogues for commercial material which could be adopted and/or adapted. It will be time and money well-spent.

Some further aspects of presentation

There still remain one or two things that should be said about the handling of visual aids generally in group focusing sessions. First, two points which apply overall. No matter what kind of pictures are being used, projected or not, it is essential that the learner can see the aids

122

clearly. If pictures are being projected for a large group, for example, the projectionist should herself go to several different positions in the room and check beforehand that the children to be sitting there will be able to see well. Or again, if ordinary pictures are to be used, the teacher should check in advance that there are adequate facilities for presenting them. All too often the teacher herself holds the picture, trying at the same time to point to things, with the result that her arm completely blocks the view for at least some of the children. A proper picture stand is an advantage or the visual should be made to hang from a hook on the wall or be pinned to the wall. If a set of flip-over pictures is used it is helpful to put them on an easel-board so that they can be easily turned and made to hang over the back. Again the teacher must ascertain that all the children in the group are in a position to see everything clearly.

Some attempt should be made to vary the techniques of presentation. We have already seen something of the range of possible visuals and have considered a few techniques, particularly with regard to 'hardware'. Teachers should try to ring the changes as much as possible. A story, for instance, could be told initially by means of cut-out figurines, repeated by using flip-over pictures and told yet again by a combination of projector and tape-recorder. Each presentation has the freshness of something new to the children although, perhaps with different emphases on the teacher's part, the same language work is being covered. This variety of technique has at least two useful purposes, one to keep the interest of the learners in work which has to be covered again and again, and two to give opportunities to the teacher for stressing different facets. Each kind of aid has its own particular contribution to make to the learning process.

Secondly, concerning the use of ordinary visuals in particular, there are a few further points which could be mentioned about the techniques themselves.

1. *Focuser*

In the discussion on kinds of visual aids, mention was made of the picture which contained several talking-points for focusing on, as opposed to the series of pictures each of which illustrated one point. A useful technique for helping the children to fix their attention on one area at a time is to make use of a focuser. It is a piece of card or manilla paper, the same size as the picture, with one quarter cut away. The visual should be designed so that there is a point of focus in each quarter. The focuser is placed on top and is turned and swung round to reveal each quarter in turn.

2. *Sets and series*

The Donn Byrne Picture Composition pictures have already been referred to in Chapter 5. These illustrate another useful technique. There are four sets of flip-over pictures and it is necessary to display all four at the same time. They depict several series of events either as bases for stories or for general language work on ordering. If the top picture in each set is shown then the four together constitute a series. If all the pictures are turned over then the second series appears, and so on. It is useful to number both the sets and the pictures in the sets for speed and ease of arrangement. The number of sets, of course, need not necessarily be four.

3. *Magnet-board*

This is really an essential piece of apparatus for language work although with less ease of movement the teazel/flannel-graph can serve the same purpose. It is so useful to be able to mount the cut-out figurines and to move them about. The reticulated figure is made by fixing the head and limbs by means of clips such as the two-pronged paper-clip where the prongs are pushed through the hole and then bent back. This allows the body parts to be manipulated and work can be done on language to describe various actions. The figures can be clothed with paper garments, another source of language work.

A story can be made particularly interesting with the teacher building up the scenes in front of the children. Specially prepared background sheets can be used or the teacher can outline the backgrounds with chalk.

Another advantage of magnet-board work is that it allows for much enjoyable participation by the children themselves. They love to manipulate the figurines. And these can be used for many purposes besides that of illustrating the theme for which they were originally intended. For instance the original story characters can be used to help with the concepts and language of mathematics.

One idea is to have a background sheet showing two ladders. A child could be asked to place X on one ladder and Y 'nearer the top/bottom' of the other. Or more precisely, the instructions could be to place X 'on the third step' and Y 'two steps higher' and so on. The magnet-board is an excellent gadget for practice with the language of position generally, for example, 'at the left' 'in the middle' and prepositions such as 'behind', 'in front of' and 'next to'.

4. Chalkboard

There is still a place in this sophisticated age for the old-fashioned chalk and board. The artistically gifted teacher can build up her pictures this way, keeping up the interest by saying such things as, 'What is this going to be?' or 'Where shall I put the X?'. Even a story could be unfolded in this way, though unless the teacher were very expert, it would tend to be a slow procedure, and the magnet-board figurines are probably better for this. However, in work such as that described for the last version of *The Naughty Cat* in Chapter 6, free-hand drawing by the teacher might help the guessing strategies.

For the not so gifted teacher there is always the match-stick figure, a quick and easy device for illustrating all kinds of things. Teachers should try to improve their techniques in this respect. See the suggestions for further reading.

Conclusion

Again the list is by no means exhaustive. Teachers will be able to add many more ideas of their own, though any list will be constrained to a large extent by the kinds of resources available and the purposes for which they are wanted. Aim, aid and technique are very closely related. In consequence it has been difficult to divide this chapter into mutually exclusive sections. Inevitably something of technique has appeared beside kind and purpose and vice versa. But perhaps this is all to the good. The study of language teaching, no less than the study of language itself, demands focusing on both the individual components and those components as they react upon one another in use.

Further Reading

Coppen, H. *Wall Sheets, their Design, Production and Use* National Committee for Audio-Visual Aids, 33 Queen Anne Street, London, W.1

Dale, E. *Audio-Visual Methods in Teaching—Revised* Holt, Rinehart and Winston 1965

Phelps, R. *Display in the Classroom* Blackwell 1969

Taylor, J. E. *Materials in the Classroom* Blackwell 1971

Corder, S. P. *The Visual Element in Language Teaching* Longman 1966

Lee, W. R. and Coffen, H. *Simple Audio-Visual Aids to Foreign Language Teaching* Oxford University Press 1964

Trowbridge, N. E. *The New Media Challenge* Macmillan 1974

Also

A Catalogue of Wallcharts (Educational Foundation for Visual Aids, 33 Queen Anne Street, London W.1)

8
The Centre of Interest:
An Integration of Learning

Introduction

Most teachers are familiar with the word 'project'. It suggests an integration of activities geared to a specific topic or theme. In a sense this is what is meant here by 'centre of interest'. The latter term is preferred because it is felt that 'project' has acquired, over the years, certain overtones of sophistication which are inappropriate in the present context. Also the word 'centre' is a constant reminder of the focusing which is being advocated. The centre of interest indicates a focusing on a theme which becomes the topic of several different activities. It forms a unit of learning provided by a cross-section of the curriculum.

Throughout this book the important link between experience, thought and language has been stressed. Here, in the use of a technique which presents an integration of experience aimed at generalising the learning of skills and concepts, the importance of language as a servicing agent must be emphasised yet again. It must also be pointed out that the centre of interest is not only serviced *by* language, it also serves as a kind of super vehicle or omnibus for the further learning of language itself.

Once again much of the success of such an activity depends on the initial planning by the teaching team. The theme, activities, materials and language must all be carefully considered. If each area of the curriculum has been studied and analysed from the point of view of its objectives and the activities and materials available, and if furthermore, the language which all this demands has been put together in an agreed school checklist, then the planning of a centre of interest is made very

127

much easier since so much of the work has already been done. What *is* new is the topic which is being introduced and extra thinking will have to be done, first on the choice of topic and second on the selection of suitable areas of the curriculum in which to work, making sure that the activities, materials and techniques used are really made to serve the theme. Finally some careful thought must be given to the special language, the vocabulary and perhaps formulae, which is particularly appropriate to the topic and may be new to the children. An example of a centre of interest, catering for children in the second phase of development follows. It is assumed that the teaching team has already done its 'homework' on the curriculum and that there is a school language checklist.

Initial planning

The first task is to choose the topic. To some extent even this part of the work has been made easier because there is already a section on 'Categories of Experience' (see Chapter 3, p 51) in the school checklist. The third item from this is selected, 'The Street—shops and other buildings, vehicles and activities'. This is a fairly wide theme, offering lots of scope for interesting and fruitful work.

Next the areas of the curriculum have to be decided upon and these are as follows:

> Outside visit
> Story
> Creative activities
> (a) painting and modelling
> (b) role-playing
> Singing and movement
> Pre-reading

Before going into the detailed planning of activities, materials and techniques in each of these areas, it is necessary to decide on a broad plan of procedure. The decisions at this stage are:

1. Select a particular street near the school and agree on the main features to be focused on.

2. Prepare the children for the visit by the use of a picture (projected) for all to study together and sets of small pictures showing the focal component parts, for use with small groups before and after the visit. All pictures should be as representative of the real street to be visited as possible. This means that Miss X and Mrs. Y, the artists/photographers on the staff, have to devise/take the pictures.

3. A tentative language checklist for the centre of interest will be drawn up at this point. It should cover the language to be focused on in connection with the pictures and certain items selected from the school checklist so that language of general applicability is practised and also language relevant to the areas of the curriculum chosen.

4. All the children and all the adults visit the street together. There will be constant chatting about the scene, both still and passing, with the teachers bearing in mind the features and language they have already focused on, continually helping the children to label, qualify, relate and classify. The teachers must also note any new features which particularly interest the children so that they can be focused on later.

5. The language checklist will be revised to bring in selected new language resulting from the visit and each teacher will have a copy of this.

Let us suppose now that these plans have been put into operation and our imaginary team have reached point 5. Each teacher has a copy of the following:

THE CENTRE OF INTEREST LANGUAGE CHECKLIST

The Street

Nouns	*Verbs*	*Adjuncts*	*Other structural words*
shop	cross	busy	he/she/it/they
street	drive/drove	wide	who
supermarket	buy/bought	fast	and
pay-desk	sell/sold	high	in front of/behind
post-office	work	slow (ly)	into
building	clean	quick (ly)	
bus	walk	red	
van	run/ran	green	

The Street

Nouns	Verb	Adjuncts	*Other structural words*
vehicle	go/went	clean	
traffic-warden	stop	dirtý	
window-cleaner	be	full	
traffic-lights	do/did	empty	
conductor	tell/told	hurt	
bell	make/made	here	
ticket	pretend	there	
accident	sing/sang	up	
ambulance	begin	down	
hospital	fit	together	
man	keep	nearly	
lady	crash	finished	
boy		again	
people		loud (ly)	
coat		quiet (ly)	
paint		not	
brush			
clay			
story			
song			
jigsaw			

Basic sentence types

Question with 'who', e.g. Who's this/that?
Exclamation Oh dear!

Formulae

Topic do the shopping
have an accident
Fares, please!
General Excuse me.
Good morning.
Story once upon a time
suddenly
Pre-reading (jigsaw) fits here/there/in

Rules and patterns

Nouns the 's' plural
Verbs the irregular is/are
was/were

130

```
        phrasal   get on/off
        the regular past —ed
Adjuncts   comparative and superlative, e.g.
            higher/wider
            highest/widest
Sentences  extension by phrase—every day
           negative   not/n't
```

The reader will notice that the same framework has been used here as that for the language checklist in Chapter 3. It must be remembered that the language which appears on the centre of interest list is not the *only* language which will be used in the field at large. This is the language chosen for focusing on and it could be more or less than that shown here. It must be understood too that the selection should not be a haphazard matter. If teaching teams are working together and keeping proper records of what is covered, then teachers will know how to use each new centre of interest to the best advantage.

For example in this particular topic, it is supposed that when the children actually went into the street they witnessed an accident, something the teachers in their initial planning had not bargained for. This would cause tremendous excitement. The children would want to recall and retell the events. For this they would need new vocabulary such as 'accident', 'hurt' and 'ambulance' and a way of expressing past time, so the simple past tense of the verb could be focused on.

Concerning the vocabulary of this list as a whole, the reader might like to try picking out those words which are particularly relevant to the topic and those which have been selected from the imaginary school checklist. The word 'supermarket', for instance, is obviously to do with the topic, 'lady' is a word of very general applicability, and 'jigsaw' is a word used in the area of pre-reading.

Further planning

With the centre of interest now launched by means of focusing with pictures and an outside visit, the team are ready, armed with their language checklist, to proceed to the work in the other areas of the curriculum chosen. They may decide to keep the children as one group, moving from one area of the curriculum to the next or they may decide to divide them into smaller groups with either all the groups doing

131

everything at some stage or different groups doing different things. Another possibility is for some activities to be community sessions, such as story and role-play, and the rest to be done in small groups. Again it has to be decided whether all the teachers will cover all the areas of the curriculum or certain members of the team take responsibility for certain areas. Let us suppose now that our imaginary team decides upon the following:

1. Story, role-play and singing and movement will be community activities.

2. Mrs. X will be responsible for all the story-telling but the team as a whole will help to select, adapt and/or devise the stories.

3. Miss Y will be responsible for all the singing and movement but the team as a whole will help to select, adapt and/or devise the songs and movement sequences.

4. The community happenings will be conducted by the whole team in the usual way.

5. Each teacher will cover painting and modelling and pre-reading activities with her own group and be responsible for her own planning.

With this broad blueprint the team sets to work and the activities, materials and techniques are planned so that the topic starts to pervade all these areas of the curriculum with all the language of the checklist being focused upon in different ways over and over again. Let us look in some detail at the area of story-telling.

STORIES

The materials selected are as follows:

(a) Two stories taken from books in the book-corner, one of which has to be simplified.

(b) One story devised using the King Street children in the Scope materials (See further reading).

(c) Four stories specially devised with reference to the street visited.

The techniques to be used are:

(a) Story to be built up by means of manipulating figurines on the magnet-board.

(b) Series of flip over pictures to be displayed and discussed.

(c) Sets of 'frames' to be shown on the overhead projector with accompanying sound-effects on tape.

The four devised stories are as follows:

1. *The Big Red Bus*

The big red bus is going quickly. Here is a bus-stop. There are people waiting. The bus is stopping. Now the people are getting on. The conductor is ringing the bell. He is walking up the bus. He is saying, 'Fares, please' and the people are buying their tickets. A man wants to get off. The bus is stopping and the man is getting off. The big red bus is going again. Now it is far away.

2. *The Window-cleaner*

This is a post-office. It is a high building. The window-cleaner is working. He is cleaning the windows. They are very dirty. The bucket is full of water. The window-cleaner is high up. Oh dear! I hope he won't fall.

3. *The Accident*

The traffic-lights were green and the vehicles were going. Suddenly a dog ran in front of a car. There was an accident. The car stopped quickly. There was a van behind the car. It crashed into the car. The man in the van was hurt. The ambulance came and took him to hospital.

4. *The Naughty Dog*

Once upon a time a lady went into a big shop. It was a supermarket and it was very busy. The lady had an empty basket but soon it was full. She bought fruit and vegetables and bread and milk. Then she bought some meat. She put the meat in her basket and went to the pay-desk. Suddenly a dog ran into the supermarket. Oh dear! He saw the lady's meat. He ran quickly and took the meat out of her basket. The lady didn't see him. She walked out of the shop and went home in the bus. She had no meat for her dinner. What a naughty dog!

There are two points which are worth noting about these stories. The first is that there is some attempt at progression. The first two, written in the present tense, are easier and can be related as commentaries to series of pictures. The last two, in the past tense, are not quite so easy to follow from pictures. Of these the third is probably easier than the last. It matches what the children actually saw and they would already have been helped to relate this after the event. There is one example of extension by phrase in the sentence, 'The man *in the van* was hurt'. The last story is a piece of fiction begun in the typical story manner, 'once upon a time' and the language is more complex altogether.

The second point is that such language as does appear in the checklist is one of two kinds. Either it is already well-known to the children, for example, the words 'fruit' and 'vegetables' and the structure, 'this is a ——' and the 'ing' from the verb, and it is used here by way of revision, or it has not been focused on before and is suggested to the teaching team by the nature of the story. Expressions like 'far away', 'I hope ——', 'went home' and 'what a ——!' have been deliberately introduced because the opportunities arose. They could be added to the centre of interest checklist along with those which are bound to arise in the other areas of the curriculum. They should be kept together in a separate place for focusing upon later, perhaps in other centres of interest.

Other areas of the curriculum

Perhaps the above will serve to illustrate the kind of detailed planning that must be done and the use of the checklist but something will now be said briefly about each of the other fields of activity in turn.

1. *Singing and movement*

It will be remembered that our imaginary team decided to do the singing and movement also as community activities. Action songs such as the following are devised (to *Mulberry Bush* modified):

> The wheels on the bus go round and round,
> Round and round, round and round,
> The wheels on the bus go round ahd round,
> All day long.
> The bell on the bus goes ping, ping, ping,
> Ping, ping, ping, etc.

The movement sessions are sometimes accompanied by music and sometimes not, for example:

(a) This is the way we walk/run/drive to school (sung to the tune of *Mulberry Bush*).

134

(b) Traffic moving and stopping with a child as policeman directing traffic or as the traffic-lights, holding up the appropriate colours.

2. Creative activities (role-playing)

These are in the form of community happenings. It is decided for some of the work to link with the story-telling. The stories of *The Window-cleaner* and *The Naughty Dog* can be easily adapted for instance. The following new idea is tried out, where the monitor instructs and questions the actress as well as commenting to the children.

THE WINDOW-CLEANER

A teacher appears with a bucket.

Monitor   Here is the window-cleaner.
              He is in the post-office. It's a high building.
              He's going to clean the windows.
              They are very dirty.

Here she may question the community in the usual way.
The monitor then shouts to the window-cleaner who pretends not to hear.

Monitor   Open the window.

She repeats more loudly.

Monitor   Open the window.

The actress pretends to open the window with some effort.

Monitor   Now come outside.
              Stand on the ledge.

The actress pretends to be afraid of the height. She looks down and wobbles.
The monitor uses the words in the original story as she comments to the community.

Monitor   I hope he won't fall.

She speaks again to the window-cleaner.

Monitor   Careful! Stand up straight.
              Is your bucket full?
Actress   Yes, it is.
Monitor   Have you got your cloth?
Actress   Yes, I have.
Monitor   Is the window very dirty?

Actress	Yes, it is.
Monitor	What are you going to do?
Actress	I'm going to clean the window.

The monitor speaks to the community again.

Monitor	Let's watch the window-cleaner.
	Now he is working, etc.

3. Creative activities (painting and modelling)

One teacher decides to do a wall-frieze of the street. This involves her whole group and it brings in not only painting but also collage. The children are encouraged to be responsible for different parts of the street and are asked to check with the real street as they come and go to school, for example:

Teacher	Did you see a traffic-warden?
Child	Yes, I did.
Teacher	Where did you see him?
Child	Car.
Teacher	Did you see him beside a car?
Child	Yes, I did.
Teacher	Say, 'beside a car'.
Child	Beside a car.
Teacher	Say, 'I saw a traffic-warden beside a car', etc.

The teacher could then go on to ask, 'What was he doing/wearing, etc.?' It is not often realised just how much language work can be brought into an activity of this kind. In passing it is useful to note that the three stages of a practical activity give practice with different verb tenses. Before the work begins the children can say what they are *going to do*. While it is in progress they can say what they *are doing* and when it is complete what they *did*.

Another teacher decides that the members of her group should each paint a different building, vehicle and person. These will eventually be mounted under the headings:

(a) Buildings in the Street
(b) Vehicles in the Street
(c) People in the Street

and they will become useful visual aids for further language work.

136

Modelling with clay and plasticine is attempted by some of the groups, each selecting a particular scene in the street and building up the component parts. Like the figurines for the magnet-board models can be moved about and the children enjoy ringing the changes, with the teacher helping them to express what they are doing.

4. *Pre-reading*

All the teachers are concerned with visual/motor skills, left/right orientation, auditory/speech skills and sequencing. Within this framework it is up to each of them to plan how best the centre of interest can serve and be served.

For example, one teacher decides to make strip books for work on 'alike/different'. The objects will all be things to do with the street. Another makes discrimination sheets where the children have to match cut-out pictures of shops, vehicles, etc., on to strips of pictures. A further idea used is the large picture with a hidden picture in it for the children to find. These are only a few examples of what is done. In addition, all the teachers may decide to make use of a jigsaw of the street. This is why the word 'jigsaw' appears in the checklist, and the expression, 'fits here/there/in'. Putting together a jigsaw is an extremely useful activity as it involves so many skills.

The reader might like to think about how some of the other language in the checklist not included in the brief descriptions above, could be brought into the work. For instance the phrase, 'every day' could be practised when talking about the work of the various people in the street and words like 'higher' and 'highest' can be used in pre-reading sequencing activities. The skill of the teacher lies in matching experience and language and in arranging things so that the one serves the other and vice versa.

Conclusion

An important thing to remember about the centre of interest is that the most careful planning cannot take care of everything. As the work progresses teachers will find many new and exciting things to be explored which they had not previously thought of. They will also find that some of the things they had planned, turn out to be not very practicable or useful. There must be flexibility and a readiness to adapt on the part of all and there must be frequent meetings to assess progress. In particular there should be careful judgement of the point at which to stop. A centre of interest will cease to be so if the motivation drops.

Perhaps the most important features of this work are the integration of activities and the necessity for team-teaching. These things have been stressed throughout. Even when teachers are working with small groups on their own, their planning is done in the light of what others are doing and the use of the language checklist, which is shared by all, is a real integrating factor.

The way of working described here is by no means the only method. Some possible alternatives were indicated earlier. There are many variables which can affect the kind of procedure chosen, such as the nature of the topic itself, the organisation in the school and the accommodation available, the needs of the particular children involved etc. One thing not suggested, and this could have been done within the scheme presented in this chapter, is the possibility of the progressive build-up of language. For instance after the visit and picture focusing sessions where the initial checklist is revised, the new language from the stories could be incorporated and used for the next activity such as role-playing. This in turn would yield more new language which could be used in singing and movement, and so on. But care would need to be taken in controlling the amount of new material presented.

Whichever method is adopted, it is useful to file the final checklist for future reference along with some notes on the work as a whole. The importance of record-keeping has been stressed before. It is essential in connection with both composite work and individual and it is also essential to have records of the individual language progress of the children. It is hoped that this chapter where a centre of interest for children has been described to illustrate what teachers can do to help the integration of learning, will also serve to some extent, to integrate the main features of this book.

Further Reading

Scope Stage 1 An Introductory English Course for Immigrant Children (Longman Books for Schools 1969)

138

9

Summary and Possible Implications

What the book highlights

Based on the belief that language is an important tool of learning, with an underlying code which has to be cracked, and that learning is a matter of both making discoveries and forming habits, the approach of Field and Focus and its development through three phases for the second-language learner which is described in the second chapter, has served as a framework for the various techniques discussed in the rest of the book.

There is undoubtedly a great deal more that could have been said about the techniques and there are many others which have not been touched on at all. But perhaps what has been covered has been sufficient to highlight the main features of the teacher's task. Chapter 3 introduces and describes the language checklist, without which it is felt, the work can become haphazard and lacking in direction. It is important to remember that the list should be the result of careful focusing by the whole teaching team on the demands of the field, a field which itself has been planned so that both in content and extent it is appropriate to the learners concerned. Used properly, the checklist helps the teacher to (a) control the input of learning (b) check learning progress and (c) assess the level of the child.

Chapter 4, which describes the use of the language 'kit-bag', attempts to illustrate what is involved when focusing on language with children in the very early stages of learning the second language. It also tries to show the usefulness of two or more adults working together and acting as foils for one another. It is worth stressing in passing that these adults need not always be teachers. They need not even be adults in the usual meaning of the word. They could be English-speaking children whose fluency in the language is 'adult' compared with that of the second-language learners concerned.

There is a sense in which the contents and use of the language 'kit-bag' demonstrate the whole approach advocated here, experience given to quicken thought, and language, both structure and vocabulary, taught to help the ordering and expression of experience. The teacher should find that the kind of thinking she has to do in preparing and using the language 'kit-bag' will continue to influence and help her work long after the child's increasing fluency makes the bag as such no longer necessary.

The community happening dealt with in Chapter 5, besides emphasising the need for large group activities which give a sense of togetherness particularly at the Initial orientation stage, serves to point up the importance of role-play in general and the value of slowing down and monitoring experience which is carefully matched with appropriate language. The knowledge of social concepts in the new world about the child and the development of his self-concept within this world, are just as vital as his understanding of physical concepts, and role-play helps towards this end.

So also does the story-telling and related techniques with which Chapter 6 is concerned, linked to the careful selection and use of illustrative materials as discussed in Chapter 7. But all this work has many aims in view. Sometimes the emphasis is on thought development with language used as a tool and sometimes it is on the learning of the expression system with materials used to give meaning so that thinking helps speaking.

Finally in the previous chapter, an attempt is made to show how several of these techniques can be incorporated in the centre of interest whose purpose is to integrate the learning in various areas of the curriculum, using language as the 'servicing agent' throughout. It is here that the importance of teachers working together as a team is really apparent, but it is hoped that this way of working has been shown to be vital to the entire approach.

Reading and writing, the next stage

The reader may have wondered why, in a book about language, so little has been said concerning the skills of reading and writing. The reason is not that these things are considered unimportant but that it is felt that they more properly belong to the next stage. It has, however, been suggested that a start could be made in the third of our phases, as a continuation of the pre-reading activities begun during the intensive oral work of the second phase. Some word recognition and reading and putting together sentences which can be spoken fluently, could be tackled at this time. But it must be remembered that the breakthrough to fluency is still very recent and it is likely that this oral fluency must be better established and increased before an attempt is made to 'break through to literacy'. It is, incidentally, useful to note that when this is begun, the materials of the same title are extremely useful (see references). For instance the child can put words together without the chore of writing the letters. The words are prepared for him. It is worth noting also that the view of language learning taken in this book seems to support that held by the writers of these materials in their approach to literacy.

Further implications

The mention of the next stage is a reminder that the approach to the learning of English as a Second Language in early education which is described here, must be seen in the context of education in general. There are things implied which many people will question because they suggest what may be radical changes in thinking and methodology for lots of teachers and schools. Let us, in conclusion, consider a few of these implications. Even if we raise and do not attempt to answer the questions, some useful pointers for research may be given for those who are in a position to take the matter further. It might be helpful to think first about the implications for the teachers and those who educate them and second, about what is implied for local authorities, the policy-makers and those who make educational provision.

(a) Teachers and their education

It is essential that, in addition to learning the work of the good teacher of young children, the student must have a firm grounding in matters of culture and language and particularly the ways in which these things affect learning. In the multi-cultural society the teacher has to be pedagogue, anthropologist and linguist all at the same time and her education must reflect these disciplines. There should be more applied linguists in colleges which educate teachers, prepared not only to educate the students but also to initiate research into better ways and means, working closely with teachers in schools so that the fruits of this research have an immediate bearing on the practice there and on the training of new teachers.

It is vital that the teachers appointed to first schools should be educationists of the highest calibre, people with open minds prepared to experiment and to work with others as part of an expert team. It is essential also that they see themselves as part of a wider team which extends downwards to the nursery schools and upwards to the middle and higher levels. A child does not become another being as he moves from one stage to the next. He is the same child with continuing needs which require a continuity of care and attention.

While this holds for all aspects of the child's development it is particularly important for the development of language which plays such a vital role throughout the entire range of his education. All teachers must be alerted to this fact and trained to cope efficiently at whatever level and in whatever subject they may be working. But for the teachers of young children whose responsibility in this area is probably greatest of all, there should be particular emphasis on language development.

It is suggested, for example, that work should be done with these teachers comparing first language acquisition with second language learning. For too long now education has suffered from two opposing myths which must be scotched once and for all. The first is that the five-year-old can pick up a second language in the same manner in which he acquired his first, simply by being exposed to it. This has led to the present situation where very little positive tuition in oral language is given by teachers in first schools. They give the odd correction here and there and help to some extent by labelling new objects, as the mother of a young baby will do at home. What is not understood is that this haphazard practice is just not sufficient for many children. The child will never again be in the position of the baby acquiring his first language. That 'critical' period between the ages of two and four when the child is like a sponge in the way in which he absorbs language, has gone never to return. The child from a home where the language is not that of the school has to be taught a second language and made conscious of his learning. And time is at a premium.

The ironic thing is that many of the people who advocate the laissez-faire approach to the learning of a second language, lay great store on the value of the peer-group. They believe that the child will soon pick up the language from the English-speaking children around him. In the same breath these people will ask, 'Why all the fuss anyway about teaching language to "foreigners"? Some of our own British children could do with help.' And how right they are. But the point is, these British children are often the very ones from whom the second-language learner is supposed to be picking up his English!

The second myth is that first language acquisition and second language learning are completely different and should be treated as such. This has resulted in the growth of second-language teaching techniques which, until recently, have reflected very strongly the tenets of behaviouristic psychology. To many teachers in this country and especially those in first schools, the whole ethos is anathema and entirely inappropriate to the education of young children, the net result being once again, that no tuition of the second language is done in the early stages of school.

Teachers have to be shown first that mother-tongue acquisition and second-language learning, even though not the same, do have certain things in common which should give some clues to what the teacher can do to help, and second that language learning, like any other kind of learning, is a matter of both making discoveries and forming good habits, each of which must be catered for.

What now requires to be done, and that very urgently, is first of all a reappraisal of this whole situation and secondly an all-out attempt to educate teachers in training and to re-educate teachers in service, along these lines. Teachers should be told about the steps of language acquisition that the young baby goes through, for instance, so that they can study them with reference to the second-language learner. The ability of the child to imitate, to make analogies and to generalise, should be recognised and fostered by appropriate provision and techniques on the part of the teacher. The notion that learning begins in actual limited situations and develops with a gradual widening of experience should also be noted and acted upon. The current obsession with creativity has often blinded teachers to the fact that one cannot be creative in oral language without the possession of a skill and that this skill is not merely a matter of maturation. Like the skill of reading it has to be taught.

Teachers should be shown also that there are things about the techniques of teaching a second language which can be adapted and made appropriate to the education of the young child. Through guided and directed play and the use of apparatus and toys already part of the school environment, the teacher can help the child to focus on the particular things about language which she knows to be important for him. A special language course is probably not necessary for the young child, but it is necessary that the teacher should have some guidelines. This is the idea behind the language checklist. It pervades everything that is done.

Finally it is suggested that teachers should be helped to compare cultures and languages so that they are in a better position to understand and to cope with 'interference' of learning. There is a certain amount of literature on this to which teachers' attention can be drawn. In addition there are numerous courses and conferences on the multi-cultural society organised by colleges, the Department of Education and Science, local authorities and other bodies such as the Community Relations Commission. Not all teachers of young children realise that these things are relevant to *them*. Perhaps a better awareness of the issues involved might do something to remedy this. Teachers need to learn what they need to know.

(b) *Local authorities*

In-service training of teachers must be a priority for the local education authorities. The education of teachers cannot be left to the

144

colleges which have to take a more general overall view of the matter. Each area has its own particular problems and the teachers appointed there must be educated in this context. There should be at least one adviser who is competent to organise courses on the teaching of children from a variety of cultures and a strong component of these courses should be the teaching of language. Ideally there should be an advisory team so that teachers of all age-groups should really be catered for not only in the matter of special courses whether centre or school-based, but also in the matter of on-going visits and real professional help on the spot. All too often, as things stand, there is one adviser/inspector who is responsible in a vague, umbrella fashion for the Teaching of English as a Second Language or the Education of Immigrants or, worse than this, the Education of the Disadvantaged which is supposed somehow to cover children of other cultures. He/she is usually so over-burdened by the enormity of the administrative load, especially if the post also carries responsibilities for general inspection as it often does, that there is no time or opportunity for the real business of advising and training, even if this super-person were capable of helping adequately the nursery, primary and secondary teacher.

When is some authority somewhere going to be enlightened enough to act upon the recommendations made as a result of national inquiries? The notion of an advisory team of this kind was mooted by the Select Committee on Race Relations some time ago. It is not a matter of new appointments but one of more sensible use of personnel already employed so that the very real expertise which exists in isolated pockets all over the country, is recognised, given a channel for its expression and made to serve the common good.

The local advisory team, which should be representative of all levels of education, should work closely with the people in colleges doing the initial training of teachers and there should be joint research projects on various policies and methodologies. The educational provision in schools should be examined critically and changes brought about courageously and vigorously if they are seen to be necessary. Questions must be asked and honestly answered. For instance, can one teacher, no matter how understanding, knowledgeable and competent, cater adequately for the needs of thirty children or more, of whom a large proportion have very little idea of the language used in school or the cultural values and norms that go with it, and who may at the same time come from a variety of ethnic groups?

This question has been asked many times in the context of the older child. The answer is usually, 'No' and various solutions have been found. In the context of this book should those responsible for the education of young children not be asking the same thing? Can the teacher of the young child cope any better than that of the older in this respect and might it be that by our persistent refusal to see a problem at the lower end of the educational ladder we have not only aggravated but possibly caused the problems at the upper end, many of which the recent Bullock Report has brought to light?

There are a few authorities where a positive line has been taken with children at an early level and some excellent work has been done. Bradford, for example, has its special centres and Birmingham has peripatetic teachers who work with the youngest children but this work still lies uneasily within the context of the schools as a whole and within that of education across the country in general. What is needed is something much more widespread and radical, involving new thinking, experiment, and redeployment of such resources as are available for the education of the youngest children in our schools.

In the Foreword it was suggested that the ideal solution might be some kind of bilingual education, and experiment should certainly be attempted along these lines. In the shorter term, better ways of dealing with the second language as a medium from the start, should be sought and tried. The approach suggested by this book is a case in point. It requires to be tried in a multi-cultural school which is prepared to work a system of gentle phasing-in to the full school curriculum. It needs a very good pupil/teacher ratio and teachers who are willing to work as a team, drawing upon the resources of other adults and English-speaking children in the community. It also needs 'an excellent home/school liaison scheme. Furthermore, there has to be both understanding and approval of what is happening, in the upper levels of the same school and in the schools to which the children will go eventually so that teamwork of the vertical kind is in operation as well. Children given this kind of start will not retain their advantage if it is not fostered and followed up by the teachers who have to deal with them later. This is a vitally important point which has been all too often overlooked. There should probably be exchange of staff between those who work in the 'preparatory' department and those who work in the later stages. This way teachers would come to see the things which make for real continuity and progress.

It is realised that this still leaves many questions unanswered. How multi-cultural does a school have to be, for instance, to justify having a preparatory department of this kind? And would it be only for non-English-speaking children or should West Indian and British dialect speakers be included? Are there some schools in fact where all the children need special help in the beginning?

These and many other questions, particularly of organisation, cannot be answered at this stage but they are the kind of issues which authorities should be raising while they seek for better ways and means by experiments of all types. This is the sort of work to which an advisory team at the local level could contribute and which an advisory team at national level should be co-ordinating in such a way that knowledge gained is quickly disseminated.

Perhaps the best second-language solution of all would be to put the resources into the nursery sector. With a policy of universal nursery education and the education of nursery staff, both initial and in-service, in the issues of culture and language learning many of the problems would be very much lessened. But the development of this idea must be left for another book.

Further Reading

Townsend, H. E. R. and Brittan, E. M. *Organization in Multiracial Schools* (N.F.E.R. 1972)

McKay, D. and Thompson, B. *Breakthrough to Literacy* Longman 1970

Bullock Report, Chapters 16 and 20 (See Ch. 1 for full ref.)

Report from the Select Committee on Race Relations and Immigration H.M.S.O. 1973

Appendix A

In addition to the books listed at the ends of the chapters the following books may be useful.

Abercrombie, D. *Problems and Principles: studies in the teaching of English as a second language* Longman 1954

Burroughs, G. E. R. *A Study of the Vocabulary of Young Children.* Educational Monograph Number 1, University of Birmingham School of Education 1957, reprinted 1963 and 1970

Butterworth, E. and Kinnibrugh, D. *The Social Background of Immigrant Children from India, Pakistan and Cyprus* (Scope Handbook 1, Books for Schools Ltd. Longman 1970)

Derrick, J. *Teaching English to Immigrants* Longman 1966

Gahagan, D. and J. *Telltales—Picture Stories for Language Enrichment* Evans 1975

Garvie, E. M. 'Teaching English as a Second Language at Pre-School Level' in *English in Education.* Spring 1976

Scott, R. *A Wedding Man is Nicer than Cats, Miss* David and Charles Ltd. 1971

Tansley, A. E. *Early to Number* E. J. Arnold 1970

Taylor, J. and Ingleby, T. *Number Words* Longman 1963, reprinted 1972

Also

The Ladybird Words for Number series

Appendix B

Useful addresses

Commonwealth Institute
Library and Resource Centre
Kensington High Street
London W8 6NQ

Community Relations Commission (CRC)
15/16 Bedford Street
London WC2

Centre for Information on Language Teaching (CILT)
State House
63 High Holborn
London WC1

National Book League
7 Albemarle Street
London W1X 4BB

Index

151